OWN IT!

OWN IT!
LESSONS EVERY WOMAN SHOULD KNOW

Sylvie Rodrigue

BURMAN BOOKS
MEDIA CORP.

BURMAN BOOKS
MEDIA CORP.

Published 2025 by Gildan Media LLC, aka G&D Media
by arrangement with Burman Books Media Corp.
www.GandDmedia.com

OWN IT! Copyright © 2025 by Sylvie Rodrigue and
Burman Books Media Corp. All rights reserved.

No part of this book may be used, reproduced or transmitted in any manner whatsoever, by any means (electronic, photocopying, recording, or otherwise), without the prior written permission of the author, except in the case of brief quotations embodied in critical articles and reviews. No liability is assumed with respect to the use of the information contained within. Although every precaution has been taken, the author and publisher assume no liability for errors or omissions. Neither is any liability assumed for damages resulting from the use of the information contained herein.

Edited by Lara Petersen
Cover photos by Elena Gliosca, LivePixels Photography
Book Design by Clarissa D'Costa

Library of Congress Cataloging-in-Publication Data is available upon request

ISBN: 978-1-7225-9913-3

10 9 8 7 6 5 4 3 2 1

To my daughter, Florence.
May this book inspire and
guide you as you embark on your
own exciting journey as a young woman.
The world is your oyster, ma belle.
Own it!

CONTENTS

	ACKNOWLEDGMENTS	9
	INTRODUCTION	11
1	CONQUER THE IMPOSTER SYNDROME	15
2	BE THE MASTER OF YOUR OWN DESTINY	41
3	HAVE THE COURAGE TO STEP OUTSIDE YOUR COMFORT ZONE	67
4	IGNORE THE WHITE NOISE	95
5	THE IMPORTANCE OF CHAMPIONS AND MENTORS	115
6	LIFE IS A MARATHON, NOT A RACE	133
7	YOU CAN HAVE IT ALL	153
8	KINDNESS IS YOUR ALLY: ALWAYS PAY IT FORWARD	167
	CONCLUSION	187

ACKNOWLEDGMENTS

This project would not have been possible without the love and unwavering support of my devoted husband, Paul, who has been my guiding light for the last twenty years.

I am also grateful to all my friends and family, especially my sister, Sophie, for her constant encouragement.

Finally, a special thank you to my partners and colleagues at Torys for always believing in me and for giving me opportunities I never thought were within reach.

INTRODUCTION

While my path to success has been unusual, I don't think I've lived such an extraordinary life. Many people, especially women, have faced challenges far greater than mine—professionally and personally. I am not a survivor of war or someone with a disability. I'm a white, heterosexual woman. I have friends and colleagues who are battling life—threatening diseases, managing family crises, or have suffered unbearable personal losses.

We all know someone who climbed to the top after starting with nothing. There's nothing unique about that. Countless women all over the world have inspiring stories to tell.

So, why write this book? Why tell my story?

In 2024, when the publisher approached me with this project, I was at one of the lowest points of my life. I'd hit rock bottom and was broken. I wanted to throw in the towel, give it all up, and disappear. I no longer wanted any responsibilities, nor to be the rock for those around me. It was the point of no return—or so I thought.

I was in no position to inspire or motivate anyone. Initially, I ignored the opportunity and even laughed it off, but my husband told me I shouldn't brush it off so easily. He knew in his gut that I would climb back up. That I would pull through. And that I may have another life lesson to share. He was right. Again. Writing this book was even therapeutic. Liberating.

Life has thrown me a lot of curve balls over the years. From my unknown biological roots and adoption, to my humble beginnings and leaving home at sixteen, I've faced miscarriages, broken relationships, and further personal and professional upheavals. Each lesson I've learned along the way has been a steppingstone, leading to a fulfilled, happy, and well-rounded life.

There is no doubt that I benefited from the achievements of the women who came before me. I didn't have to fight for my right to exist, to vote, or to choose my own career. I never had to choose between being a mother and a lawyer. No, my battles were very different.

Like many women, I fought the labels aimed at changing who I truly was because I didn't fit the expected mold. I was often too much. Too colorful. Too loud. By being assertive, I was deemed too aggressive. By wanting to lead, I was called too bossy, and by being confident, I was considered cocky or arrogant. And my all-time favorite label—*intimidating* because I dress in nice suits, something no one would ever say to a man. The idea that I can wear a power suit with pearls one day, but drive my pickup truck, a horse trailer, and shovel manure the next remains inconceivable.

Labels. As if women can't be multifaceted. While I'm confident and thorough in my professional life, I'm a complete bleeding heart and emotional in my personal life.

I have close friends from all walks of life—electricians, teachers, nannies, and gardeners to bankers, lawyers, accountants, doctors, and CEOs. I enjoy a hot dog with poutine one day, and sushi and champagne the next. This duality is at the core of who I am. I stopped fighting it just to fit the societal mold. I've learned to ignore the labels and own who I am. All of it.

Transforming adversity into opportunity has been one of the greatest challenges of my life, but it has also been the most rewarding success. I've learned to fight the far-too-prevalent imposter syndrome that paralyzes so many women, take control of my own destiny, and step outside my comfort zone, and I've done it more times than I can count. I learned to ignore the white noise holding me back, and I surrounded myself with the right supporters and champions. I embraced long ago that life is a marathon, not a race. Resilience and work ethic have been staples in my life, as have gratitude and paying it forward.

Each generation of women faces unique challenges. Today's challenges may not be the same as those our grandmothers faced, but they are very real. My daughter's generation, and the ones that follow, will fight their own battles and face their own mountains to climb. Many young women come to me for advice, as do young men. They struggle or feel lost and inadequate. Many believe they cannot possibly achieve what I did. They are mistaken.

I have found a way to have it all, and you can too. But you must Own It! All of it.

1

CONQUER THE IMPOSTER SYNDROME

If where we come from were a predictor of what we can accomplish professionally and personally, the world would be deprived of many fascinating and extraordinary people.

It isn't unusual to hear about successful people who came from broken homes, poverty, uneducated families, or who faced significant tragedies. They may have lacked support or guidance to navigate these challenges, yet they still broke the glass ceiling to achieve their personal and professional dreams.

How did they thrive? What distinguishes these individuals from others who are equally talented and smart but, unfortunately, allow self-doubt to dictate their future?

Human nature often drives people to limit themselves to the social and professional environment they grew up in, and to doubt their power to become who they truly want to be. The ever-so-popular parental saying, "You can do whatever you want to do, or be whoever you want to be," is meant to empower children from a young age. Unfortunately, the mantra seldom sticks once adulthood hits.

Our upbringing is a powerful mold. Many people resign themselves to what they believe they were meant to be because of where they were born, how they were raised, or the socio-economic impediments they faced as children. This is where the comfort zone lies. This is "home." Why? Because remaining among peers you perceive to be cut from the same fabric helps avoid feeling like an imposter.

In the workplace, we often see other people doing well and think they have it all together. They appear to know everything, and we assume that because we're struggling, we must not be in the right place. The reality is that they're probably thinking the same thing about us. Everyone struggles at different times in their careers or personal lives, and everyone has moments when they don't feel like they know what they're doing.

At some point in our lives, we all feel like imposters.

This is particularly true for women. Most successful and accomplished women have experienced imposter syndrome at some point in their professional or personal lives. It's remarkably prevalent and quite common for women to think they don't deserve to be where they are, or that they cannot possibly perform at the same level as others.

Whether it manifests as feelings of inadequacy, the belief that we need to be absolutely perfect in every endeavor, or the pressure to be the hardest worker, or the constant need to be like Superwoman—out of fear of being considered a fraud or a fake—it is insidious. This mindset can hinder the belief that you can accomplish anything you set your mind to. It also prevents many women from fully embracing their successes and recognizing that they have worked hard for their accomplishments and personal and professional happiness. They deserve this recognition—something most men have no problem acknowledging.

What is the solution? How can you overcome these self-doubts and truly become the person you want to be?

This topic has inspired thousands of books, and I'm not trying to reinvent the wheel. I'm neither a psychologist nor a therapist. I'm a happy and fulfilled woman—wife, mother, sister, friend, and successful lawyer. My background is rather unusual and I've spent most of my life feeling like an imposter. I still feel that way sometimes, but it has never dictated my direction, where I wanted to go, or what I wanted to achieve, both professionally and personally.

I realized early in life that these imposter feelings are deeply ingrained in my history and intertwined with my background. Acknowledging the source of these feelings and my work ethic were driving factors in overcoming the insidious self-doubts that kept resurfacing. My solution was to work tirelessly. I made a conscious decision to strive to be the best at everything I do in every aspect of my life.

The first person I needed to convince of my abilities was myself. I had to believe I could leave my past behind. Continuous learning and self-improvement require deep awareness, time, dedication, and faith. Had I not pushed through my imposter syndrome, I'd probably still be living in my hometown, not have become a lawyer, and not believe I could go any further in life. While there's nothing wrong with that path, it's not what I wanted. It wasn't my dream or my goal.

I was born on July 6, 1970, or at least that's what I was told. I don't know where I was born, nor do I know my biological parents. Biologically, I am 100 percent Irish, but where I came from remains a mystery. I was only six weeks old when my French-Canadian parents adopted me from a Catholic nursery on the south shore of Montreal. It was never a secret. I was about two years old when my adoptive mother told me I was adopted.

Because of my Irish heritage, my adoptive parents celebrated St. Patrick's Day each year in honor of these roots, despite not speaking a word of English. Then, when I was twenty-seven years old, I was told I may have been born in Dublin, Ireland, not Canada. The theory was that I may have been part of the Irish Magdalene scandal, where babies were stolen from their mothers and shipped away for adoption without consent. There was a lot of speculation and many doubts, but no certainties, despite numerous attempts to uncover the truth of the story. *My* story.

When I was thirty-six years old, I went to Dublin for the first time. It was a business trip. The elderly taxi driver at the airport thought I was local, with my black hair and green eyes. A Galway Girl, he thought. He spoke to me in the Gaelic language and was a bit thrown off when I responded with my heavy French-Canadian accent. After sharing my story with him, including the possibility that I was a Magdalene baby, he stopped the car. He announced that he had been one of the drivers who brought babies to the airport back in the day, and if I'd been one of those babies, he may have been the driver who took me to the airport to be sent away for adoption.

I was in total shock. He took me to the Magdalene building, the archives, and connected me with various resources to get my name in the system so someone could contact me should there be a match to my biological mother.

News travels fast in Ireland. Someone in Belfast had already heard about my story when I went there a few days later for a meeting. The pub, I was told, is the fastest way to communicate in Ireland! In any event, spreading the word yielded nothing.

Over the years, I developed close relationships with many friends in Ireland because of my daughter's competitive career in Irish dancing and Olympic boxing. Those activities meant spending a lot of time in Ireland. Despite making all those connections, still nothing. I still don't know who my biological mother is, or if I was really born in Ireland. I may never know my true origins. DNA testing confirmed my Irish roots, but that's the only certainty I have.

With an unresolved mystery surrounding my origins, I had a troubled start to life. This nourished deep insecurities throughout my early years fuelled my need to be in constant control and aversion to uncertainty.

My adoptive parents already had two boys a few years older than me when I came into their lives. I wasn't even the baby they intended to adopt. My mother told me that when she saw me in the crib beside the baby she was supposed to take home, she was drawn to me and chose me instead. Destiny, I guess.

A few years later, my parents adopted another daughter. Then, nine years after I became part of the family, they unexpectedly had a biological daughter. Our family of seven lived in Beloeil, a predominantly French-speaking suburb of Montreal's South Shore. No one in the family spoke English.

We were a blue-collar family. My parents didn't have an opportunity to pursue higher education. My mother stayed at home and my hard-working father did everything and anything to make ends meet, from working in trades, restaurants, retail, and sometimes as a traveling salesman.

While we didn't have much, I have some beautiful childhood memories, like camping and fishing with my dad. We often went for picnics or car rides, what my dad called a "nowhere." If it was free, we did it, as we couldn't afford to travel far or to stay in hotels. In fact, my first time on an airplane was for a business trip when I was twenty-four years old. There was none of that growing up. Flying wasn't even on my radar.

My childhood included long stretches of poverty. I remember aunts and uncles having to bring us groceries at times because we only had baloney, bread, and peanut butter to eat at home. Hand-me-down clothing from charitable organizations or the local church was a staple in our wardrobe. I often wore my brothers' clothes.

Despite my father's work ethic, he couldn't prevent a recurring pattern: having a job, losing it, accessing unemployment insurance, and then finding a new job. He filed for bankruptcy at some point. We had a house for a while, then lost it due to financial difficulties, and had to move back into a modest apartment. We moved seven times while I was growing up. My eighth move happened when I'd finally had enough of the cycle (and of my very controlling mother), so I packed my bags and left. I was just sixteen years old.

This is my background. My history. Where I come from. Those experiences led me to feeling like an imposter among my peers. I never really felt like I fit in anywhere, including at school. I didn't have the cool clothes, I couldn't go on school trips that cost money, and I wasn't one of the popular kids. I didn't have any close friends, likely because I wasn't allowed to go to anyone's house after school. My mother wouldn't allow it. I had chores waiting for at home, hence not much time to socialize. I constantly felt like an outsider, or inadequate.

From the very beginning, my instinctive response to this uneasy feeling was to push myself to be the first at everything, starting with academics. Whether in elementary school, high school, or university, I strived to get the highest grades and collect as many academic awards as I could. That's the only way I felt valued. That's also how I grew up believing I could be a lawyer one day, despite where I came from. With each award and accomplishment, I had more trust and faith in my abilities. I felt more in control.

Surprisingly, the same thing occurred in my athletic endeavors, despite being surrounded by affluent families—a world where I clearly didn't belong. To this day, I have no idea how my parents could afford my figure skating lessons, starting when I was five years old. I clearly had a guardian angel to help my parents along. How else could I have trained daily in a costly, competitive sport when there was barely any food on the table and hardly any clothes in the closet? It made no sense.

For as far back as I can remember, the only present I got all year was a pair of skates—no birthday or Christmas gifts. My parents would buy the skates at the beginning of the season in September, and then re-wrap them in December to put under the Christmas tree. Along with the skates, my mother would make a dress for my competitions. It wasn't anything fancy, as she certainly couldn't buy a new one, but she did her best with what she had.

My dad volunteered with the Skating Club and attended every training session, several times a week at 6:00 a.m. before school. He was at every competition too. He was my biggest fan and supporter. Although he had no money, his love and dedication to me left no doubt, and for that, I am grateful.

In that competitive world, I felt even more out of place than I did at school. I wasn't like the other girls. I didn't have the cool and shiny dresses, the extensive private lessons, the connections, or the out-of-rink training. I was the ultimate underdog. I loved skating and being at the ice rink. It was an escape from my reality, but I still felt like a major imposter.

Nothing could have reinforced that belief more than my experience at my first Quebec Games. I was so nervous. I remember sitting in a locker room with the other girls with all their beautiful dresses and perfect hair and makeup, looking so . . . perfect. I wasn't wearing any makeup because my mother didn't know how to apply it. And I didn't have money for makeup.

The other girls were performing a lot of advanced jumps. My parents could afford very few private lessons, which were probably subsidized. The other girls were a lot more advanced than me because they had extensive private lessons. They completely intimidated me.

Before I performed, I was overwhelmed by self-doubt. I kept asking myself, "What am I doing here?" The other girls were so well-dressed and had better skates, coaches, choreographers. Meanwhile, I sat there thinking this was going to be so embarrassing. Somehow, I managed to ignore the noise in my head. Like the angel and devil on each shoulder, I silenced the devil's voice.

Some of the other girls were so nervous that they threw up before getting on the ice. That's when I realized I had a secret weapon: the ability to control my stress and use it as fuel. I told myself, "I can do this. I'm going to do my own thing, and I'll do it for me." While I didn't have the axel jump all the other girls included in their routines, I performed my much-more modest routine as perfectly as I could.

That competition was one of the first times I truly felt like a complete imposter, and it almost paralyzed me. But when I stood on that podium, having won the silver medal, those feelings vanished. I felt accomplished and confident. I had learned an important lesson about how to conquer feelings of inadequacy the next time they returned. And, of course, they inevitably did.

Imposter syndrome resurfaced with a vengeance a few years later when I applied for law school admission after completing CEGEP (Quebec's two-year post-secondary education program). I'd wanted to be a lawyer since Grade six. When I was a child, my dad used to say he could never win an argument with me because I'd break down his reasoning. Eventually, he resorted to using "Because I'm your father" as his final answer when he needed to say no, because I would win the debate otherwise.

Becoming a lawyer was my number one goal. My dream. However, despite my near-perfect grades, I thought I wouldn't be accepted into law school. I thought "the little girl from Beloeil" didn't deserve it. I was wrong, of course. I received offers from all the universities I applied to, with scholarships and bursaries that made it possible for me to pursue post-secondary education. I decided to accept the offer from the University of Montreal. It was a big deal for me—a light at the end of the tunnel. Finally. But I was a nervous wreck about what lay ahead.

Before even starting my first semester in 1989, knowing nothing about the process of being hired as a student in a law firm, I tried to get such a position immediately. Why waste time, right? At nineteen years old, my work experiences had been as a babysitter, cashier in retail or grocery stores, administrative assistant or as a receptionist in a recycling company the previous summer. I figured I should get where I wanted to be long term as soon as possible. I sent my résumé to *the* law firm— Ogilvy Renault, the most prestigious firm in Montreal at the time. I had no idea what I was doing and didn't know you had to be a second-year law student to apply. Naturally, the firm rejected my application because it was far too premature, as I hadn't even started law school yet. They told me to try again after my second year, so I went back to my receptionist job for the summer, and in September, I began law school.

The imposter feeling was front and center. I figured all the students would be rich and come from families in the legal profession. Desperate to fit in, I used my savings to buy suits, dresses, and even a briefcase. I had no guidance, no mentorship, and no idea what I was walking into. On the first day of class, I showed up dressed like a lawyer, only to see that everyone else was wearing jeans and sweatshirts, just like in high school. I felt ridiculously out of place and adjusted my wardrobe the next day, but I still felt like an outsider.

My solution to masking the feeling was to work and study nonstop. My ticket out of poverty meant graduating with honors and getting a job at the best law firm in the city. I had no time to socialize, or so I thought. I didn't go to a single university party, which is something I regret to this day. I missed out on a fun part of adulthood because I was hyperfocused on my grades and saving money to make it to the end.

By the end of the first semester, I had the highest-grade average amongst the first-year students. I was awarded a scholarship sponsored by . . . Ogilvy Renault! The firm sent me a congratulatory letter and suggested I send my résumé, as they wanted to consider me for a student position. I replied that they already had my résumé. How ironic! When they asked me to come in for an interview, it hit me again. The imposter feeling.

I went through two interviews, still not knowing how to dress for such an occasion. Nothing in my wardrobe seemed appropriate for a law firm, and yet I was afraid of making the same mistake I'd made in September on my first day of class.

I had to decide what clothes to buy to look the part. My mind was preoccupied with telling me how I should fit in. What am I supposed to look like in a law firm? These thoughts played on repeat: What am I doing? Who am I kidding? I'm just a little girl from Beloeil. I don't even speak English properly, and I felt completely intimidated. But then I reminded myself that I'd worked hard to finish at the top of my class. I resolved to go into the interview with my chin held high, chanting, "I can do this!"

During the interview, one lawyer said, "Why on earth do you want to work at a law firm at twenty? Go travel the world. You're young and have your whole life ahead of you." I remember telling him, "Because I'm currently working as a receptionist at a recycling company. I need the money to live, and I know I'm going to end up here anyway, so why wait? I'd prefer to start now, please."

The experience was similar to the Quebec Games, where I felt like an imposter before the event, but I felt okay after it was over. I knew I belonged there. Ironically, my figure skating career made a difference in that interview. My résumé didn't showcase an ability to speak multiple languages or having traveled the world. I had my grades, my work experience, and my commitment to figure skating since age five. A key factor in my getting hired was my strong work ethic. I didn't realize the full impact of everything because I saw myself as the underdog and felt out of place, not fitting the mold my mind had created. Strangely, however, I can't say I experienced impostor syndrome very often during my summers as a law student at Ogilvy Renault or my six-month internship before being sworn as a lawyer in 1993.

Knowing they couldn't offer a position as a lawyer to all of us—that the firm would only select the best of the best—I retained this innate need to be first and have everything perfect all the time. I worked long hours, but I felt at home, and I certainly wasn't alone. My peers were often in the library late at night alongside me. We were in the same boat, all vying for the same position. Work ethics were a staple for everyone. This was my ticket out of poverty and the career I deeply wanted. Failure was not an option. I was not going to let this slip through my fingers. It was within my control to make it happen.

I remember the day they announced which of us would be offered a position as a lawyer at the end of the internship. I was extremely nervous—trembling, really—and for a minute or two, as I sat in the leather chair in a partner's corner office waiting for the news, I crumbled under self-doubt. That chair was for the imposter syndrome. Again, I said to myself, "Who am I kidding? There's no way I'm getting an offer. My fellow students are much more accomplished than I am. I don't belong in the same class as the others. I just don't fit in. This place is too prestigious for the little girl from Beloeil. I'm not going to make the cut."

And then, of course, they gave me the offer. I was just twenty-three years old. I left the office and burst out crying, not only because that was my ticket out of poverty, but mostly because my dream of becoming a lawyer and practicing in a prestigious law firm had just become a reality. I should have known better than to doubt myself. I'd been there for three years by that point. My performance evaluations had been stellar each year. I knew they valued me, yet I still had doubts. That is imposter syndrome. Only after the firm gave me the offer and I felt the accomplishment did I believe. I was quite relieved. That same day, I left the building and went to buy my first car. It turned out that most of my cohort of law students were hired as lawyers that year. It was a great group indeed.

Seven years later, at age thirty, I became a partner. Again, I'd had doubts about being promoted as a partner in such a prestigious firm. The shoulder devil whispered, "You're just this little girl from Beloeil. There's no way you'll make partner." But I did.

Imposter syndrome lingered throughout my career, most notably when I received professional awards. In 2002, when I was thirty-two years old, the editor of a Toronto-based legal magazine called *Lexpert* called to tell me I had been awarded the Top 40 Under 40 Award. This was the inaugural edition of what has become a well-known annual award recognizing the rising stars in the Canadian legal profession.

I was invited to Toronto for a photoshoot with some other award winners, all of whom were Toronto lawyers. I was the only one from Quebec, yet they asked me to appear on the cover of the magazine with them—three Toronto lawyers and me. Why? It was a complete surprise, but it also triggered my imposter syndrome once again. I thought to myself, "I'm just this little girl from . . . How is it possible that I'm on a cover of a Toronto-based legal magazine?" Coincidentally, the other female lawyer on that cover with me is now one of my partners at my current firm. Little that I knew at the time where life would eventually take me.

Fast forward to September 2006, self-doubt came back stronger than ever, and those negative feelings were front and center in the decision that profoundly transformed my life, both professionally and personally. After thirteen years of practicing solely in Quebec, I moved my law practice to the Toronto office of Ogilvy Renault so my two two-year year-old daughter and I could live with Paul and his three young boys. This uprooting triggered my imposter syndrome to resurface in various ways, threatening to paralyze life-changing decisions and deprive my daughter and me of the wonderful life we now enjoy.

Over and above the significant adjustments to my personal life, the move resulted in a lot of changes in my professional life too. Some are particularly relevant to imposter syndrome. The Toronto legal market is completely different from the Quebec market. *Cultural shock* is an understatement, and that was even while staying with the same firm.

Everything about how I interacted with colleagues and the Bench, as well as how I practiced law, was different—right down to how I dressed. It's funny how the dress code always seems to trigger my imposter syndrome. For example, the robe we wear in Quebec courtrooms is very feminine, complete with a lace collar. In Toronto, female lawyers wear the same robes as men, without the lace collar. I remember a female partner from another firm in Toronto, whom I considered a role model, telling me, "If you want to be one of us, you're going to have to dress like one of us." I recall thinking, "She's right. I'm not going to fit in. They'll always see me as the French-Canadian lawyer from Quebec—the outsider. A fake." And there it is: the impostor syndrome.

Male colleagues fuelled the feeling of inadequacy by often telling me I would never be "a real Toronto lawyer." They said I would never make it on Bay Street. That I had essentially committed "career suicide" for love.

During my transition years in Toronto, I had to fight my own insecurities every day to overcome the belief that I was an imposter. I convinced myself that I could succeed in this new market. Once again, I believed the solution was to work harder, earn my place, and, with each accomplishment, convince myself that I was not an impostor—that I truly belonged. The feelings of being an imposter were reminiscent of those I experienced in the skating change room and during my first interview with

Ogilvy Renault. While they may have been tempered after thirteen years of practice, they had not disappeared. They still spoke to me like the devil on my shoulder, but just as I had known on the podium at the Quebec Games as a child, I believed that confidence and hard work were the keys. If I believe I belong, others would believe it too.

With each success in rebuilding my professional network and reputation in a new market, my feelings of being an imposter slowly dissipated. When you do the work and reach your goals, you start to believe you can do even more. You don't have self-doubt nipping at your heels because you *know* you can succeed. This is an important step toward overcoming imposter syndrome. Given your background, those feelings may always be present, but they're not necessarily a bad thing. You don't have to let them take over. Instead, you can choose to trust yourself and your abilities.

Despite my success, the insidious feeling of inadequacy resurfaced when my current firm, Torys LLP, approached me six years after I had arrived in Toronto. In my view, Torys was *the* best firm in the country—prestigious and home to some of the top litigators. Torys was, and still is, a powerhouse for litigation with female lawyers, such as Sheila Block, Tricia Jackson, Linda Plumpton, and many others whom I considered role models throughout my career. My heroes, to be honest. These litigators were next-level, and I admired and respected each of them. I just couldn't believe they were interested in me.

Joining Torys was something I considered unattainable, and I was convinced I would never fit in. Self-doubt kicked in once again. I questioned whether the "little girl from Beloeil" was talented enough for a firm like Torys. But the truth is—*they* approached *me*, not the other way around. While imposter syndrome crept in, a stronger voice insisted: I've earned this. At first, I thought there was no way I could match their level. I had to convince myself that if they were reaching out to me, it meant I was already at their level. That inner voice grew stronger, and I eventually believed it. However, it took a long, long time.

There is no doubt that imposter syndrome has always been deeply intertwined with where I came from, and it will never completely leave me. Although it faded over time as I gained confidence, it continues to surface occasionally with each award and each success. I often wonder, how is this even possible? Being awarded twice as one of the WXN's Top 100 Most Powerful Women in Canada was no exception to this feeling. Each time I stood on stage with these ninety-nine other accomplished women, I felt I didn't belong. They had accomplished so much more than I had.

When I first step into the Supreme Court of Canada, the highest court in the country, again I thought, "What is this little girl from Beloeil doing here?" It was disbelief; however, the difference was, with age and experience, I no longer doubt my ability to get the job done.

That's the only solution to beating imposter syndrome. You don't get rid of that voice that tells you you're not good enough simply because of where you come from. Because of your background, those feelings are ingrained in you. You must believe in where you are going. That belief grows stronger and stronger the more you work toward your goals. Preparation, gaining a solid foundation of knowledge and experience, and confidence in your abilities are the keys to building your belief that you can get where you want to go.

Recognizing imposter syndrome and understanding its causes are crucial. Maybe you're young and just entering your field. Maybe you're switching jobs or just got a promotion and are nervous about failing. Maybe you're new to a city where you don't know anyone. Maybe you're completely outside your comfort zone and can only see failure in your future, whether it's in your professional or personal life.

Any of those scenarios can make you feel like an imposter or like you don't belong. The journey of self-improvement, whether it be at the beginning of your career or as you transition to the next stage, hinges on hard work and self-awareness. In other words, you are your worst enemy.

The first person you have to convince that you are exactly where you're supposed to be is yourself. Hard work and small steps toward achievement are the solutions to overcoming imposter syndrome. Will it disappear entirely? Likely not, but you can learn how to manage it, or even allow it to fuel your successes. It certainly worked for me.

I ended up developing a national legal practice, splitting my time between Montreal and Toronto each week, and benefiting from my dual civil-common law call to the bar. As daunting as moving to Toronto was, it opened doors and opportunities I would have never had if I'd remained paralyzed by imposer syndrome.

Set your goals, whether personal or professional, and aim straight as an arrow toward them. Do the hard work and stay focused. Success isn't going to fall from the sky. The only way to combat imposter syndrome, aside from ignoring the noise in your head, is to prove, not just to the world, but to yourself, that you can do it. If you don't put in the effort—whether it's for a relationship, a move to another country, or a career—it won't happen on its own. I still feel like an imposter sometimes, even at my age. My way of combating it, as I did at the skating competition, is to return to what I can do—focus on my strengths and strive to do my best.

When you do the work and have the knowledge, it isn't cockiness—it's confidence. This isn't a "fake it 'til you make it" deal. That approach won't hold, because it's built on nothing. Confidence is grounded in your accomplishments. You've already done the work and you know your abilities. This is essential to overcoming imposter syndrome.

There's also an element of not living in the past, in a sense that you can easily get trapped there if you constantly go back to where you came from, as I was guilty of doing. Thoughts like "I'm just a little girl from Beloeil. I'm never going to be a lawyer. I'm never going to be a partner. I'm never going to succeed on Bay Street. I cannot possibly be worthy of Torys," were all triggered by struggling with where I came from.

You must look ahead to where you want to go. The image of where you came from is often biased and can hold you back. The decision is yours to make, and that choice empowers you to take control of your own destiny. Embrace your journey, trust in your abilities, and let your confidence guide you forward.

2

BE THE MASTER OF YOUR OWN DESTINY

No one will take control of your life and destiny better than you. As women, we are often conditioned from birth to stand back, not push too hard or be too aggressive, and wait for opportunities to come to us. We frequently believe others are more qualified, experienced, or deserving than we are to push an idea forward. The truth is, no one is better positioned to make decisions for yourself than you. You must take control, advocate for opportunities, and believe in your ability to succeed.

The irony is not lost on me. Receiving advice about mastering your own destiny from someone whose own was uncertain from birth, and who lacked control for much of her childhood, is odd. However, it's precisely because I had no control over my circumstances from the beginning that taking charge of my life became so important. Like many adoptees, insecurities run deep when you have no biological roots, and the inexplicable feeling of rejection is omnipresent. It taints many decisions and often holds us back. Yet, these insecurities can be transformed into a powerful fuel for success.

When we set goals for ourselves and try to reach them, we sometimes impose limitations. Thoughts like: "I'm too young... it won't work... I don't have enough experience... people won't take me seriously... others can do this better than me... I'm going to fail" can surface. This mindset is different from imposter syndrome. These are just excuses that prevent us from creating own luck and opportunities. Take a chance with your own ideas or projects, rather than waiting for someone to give it to you on a silver platter in what you perceive to be a safer zone.

The fear of rejection or failure holds us back. We often hesitate to move forward and miss opportunities because we're afraid of falling flat on our faces. Yet, the only way to know whether you can do something is to take that leap of faith and embrace the risk.

You are the master of your own destiny. It sounds cliché, but it's so true. No one is going to rescue you or take charge of your life for you. No one owes you anything, not even your parents. Your dreams can become a reality if you take the reins, take charge, and make the decisions that need to be made. Put in the effort to make it happen.

The thought of taking charge and advocating for yourself can be intimidating when you're young. I've experienced this firsthand. A young person might suggest an idea in a room full of older, more experienced people, only to hear whispers afterward like, "Who does she think she is? She's just a baby. What does she know?" Of course, people will say no, but that shouldn't stop you. You'll encounter rejection, skeptics, and those who tell you that you're incapable. However, if you know what you're doing and have a solid idea, make the decision to go ahead. Be fearless. It is your choice to either hold yourself back because of others or to ignore them and go ahead. This is a choice—*your* choice—and it's in your hands.

The first major decision I made that allowed me to be the master of my own destiny was leaving home at sixteen. My home situation was holding me back, and I didn't want to follow the same path as my parents, only to end up with my future being controlled by others. I was determined to break the pattern of poverty before it was too late. It was my decision to make the scary and difficult move forward. I chose to move out.

Since I'd always wanted to become a lawyer, I set my goal and knew I had to make the right choices to get there. To get into law school, I needed scholarships. Naturally, I had a lot of insecurities, as most young people do, but I was motivated to escape that socio-economic environment, knowing no one would do it for me.

Nothing was my parents' fault. I simply knew deep down that I had to cut the cord and leave to thrive. The path was clear. I understood what I had to do, and I knew I could unlock my potential and be the best I could be. By being the top student, I knew I would attract offers from the best law firms and have the career I'd always dreamed of. It was all within my control. It felt good to be in control of my destiny for the first time in my early life.

After I left home, I moved in with my boyfriend. He helped pay the bills and was very supportive, completely devoted to me during my law school years and invested in my success. However, by the time I graduated in 1993, we had evolved in different directions. He clearly still loved me, but I had fallen out of love. It was no fault of his own; he did nothing wrong. On the contrary. I was just a different person at twenty-three than I had been at sixteen.

I still felt guilty. What kind of person depended on someone for help for eight years only to break up after becoming a lawyer? I also loved his family and was close to his mother. They had given me a true sense of family and a lot of love during a difficult time in my life, given my own family struggles. Leaving him meant "divorcing" his family as well, which felt impossible, so I procrastinated for another three years.

That was a big mistake. It only made things worse. I was unhappy and wanted other things in life. In 1996, I finally had the courage to make the hard decision and broke his heart. I left with only a small piece of luggage, leaving everything behind except a few clothes.

I moved into an apartment in Montreal with nothing more than a mattress on the floor, one plate and a few utensils, and my luggage. It was surprisingly liberating. For the first time in my entire life, I was alone, all by myself. Going to a restaurant and eating by myself was empowering. Talking walks alone was too. Everything was new. It was like being reborn.

My ex hoped we'd get back together, but the break just confirmed that I needed to move on. Breaking someone's heart isn't easy, especially when there's nothing wrong with the relationship.

There was no fighting, no disagreement, and it was clear he loved me. It was all me. I needed to move on to grow, so I did, despite the heartache. At that time in my life, I just needed to be alone.

I made similar decisions to end two other long-term relationships.

After staying single for a while, I ended my second serious relationship after three years. We lived together, and everything was fine, but our respective goals clashed. While he wanted to pursue an international career, I was approaching my 30s and wanted a child. He didn't want a family, so I took control and said we needed to split. He didn't understand why, as everything appeared to be going so well.

Making that decision was incredibly difficult. I believed success and happiness in my personal life required having a family of my own. I wanted what I wanted, and he wanted what he wanted, and he ended up getting it. He still lives abroad and achieved his goals, while I remained disciplined in my pursuit of what was important to me, and I gave up someone I loved to get it. This choice took courage and caused significant heartache for both of us. The deliberate decision to break off the relationship, even in the absence of problems, was very much in line with my desire to take charge of my destiny and make the right choices to reach my personal goals.

I then met my now ex-husband, Diego, and realized my dream of having a child—our daughter, Florence. Once again, I had to make tough decisions to remain in control of the life I wanted. Just as I was finding success in my professional destiny, Diego said he wanted to move back to his hometown, Puerto Vallarta, to join his brothers in a family business. The business was thriving, and he wanted to contribute to its success.

At first, I gave it an honest effort to find happiness there. After all, who wouldn't want to live in Puerto Vallarta? Mexico's west coast is absolutely gorgeous, and Diego's late father had played a key role in the development of this magical place back in the 1960s. I went there with Diego for a few weeks during my maternity leave, but the thought of living in a country that wasn't economically or politically stable wasn't for me. I'd worked too hard to give it all up—my independence, my financial security, our home. I just couldn't sacrifice all that to move to another country, especially with my daughter to think of. Because I didn't want to hinder Diego's opportunity either, we agreed to split. It was a blessing that we resolved everything amicably and are still good friends.

Part of my reason for wanting to stay in Canada was that I didn't want my daughter to go through what I'd been through as a child. This goes back to my early insecurity. By then, I was financially secure, I was a partner at the firm, I owned a house, and I had a child. The prospect of risking all of that for a move to Mexico felt too daunting. I had also just realized my dream of buying a lake-side cottage in North Hatley. We had a boat and friends there. I was loving my life, and I didn't want to change any of it.

Diego was happy and successful doing his thing, and I was happy doing mine. I made hard decisions to let go of that relationship so I could continue on the path of achieving my dreams, even if it meant heartaches and another painful transition. My focus always remained on the endgame rather than the obstacles or what people thought of my decisions. The determination to be the master of my own destiny guided every decision I made, leading me toward my personal and professional goals.

I followed the same mantra in my career. I never hesitated to propose projects I believed in and knew could impact my career. For example, shortly after becoming a lawyer, despite having little influence as a first-year lawyer, I sensed a wave of new litigation emerging and had an idea to propose to my firm. I approached the chair of my firm's litigation department with a suggestion to create a specialized class action practice group. My instincts were telling me that class actions would become increasingly popular in Canada, and I wanted us to get ahead of the curve and position ourselves as leaders in the field.

Despite my complete lack of experience, the department chair responded, "Good idea. Start the group, and you can chair it if you want." I ended up chairing that practice group for the entire twenty years I practiced law with Ogilvy Renault, which eventually changed its name to Norton Rose Fulbright.

Class action litigation became the focus of my career from that day on. That simple idea I shared with my immediate supervisor was pivotal in placing me in the driver's seat that took my career where I wanted it to go. I could have succumbed to the fear of rejection and waited for a senior lawyer to create this practice group, or waited for someone to ask me if I wanted to be involved, but I didn't. I had an idea, and I ran with it. I took control of my destiny.

I developed my career as a class action lawyer through deliberate decisions to engage with every possible initiative related to class actions, including involvement with the Canadian Bar Association, the International Bar Association, and the American Bar Association. I sought opportunities, found them, and acted. I got involved, offering ideas and creating new class action committees that I would lead, or asking to join existing ones. Each opportunity to speak on a panel resulted from my initiative—not someone asking me to do it. I volunteered because I was the one driving my career forward.

Of course, I sought guidance and advice along the way. I had tons of mentors and champions to support me, but the ideas, the plan, and what I needed to do all came from me. I held the reins. The desire to stay in control may stem from my adoption and the insecurities that came with it. Nevertheless, it served my career well. I refused to depend on others to determine my next steps. This was my life, and I was in control.

How I took control of my destiny couldn't have been better illustrated than through the hardest life decision I had to make after I met my husband, Paul, in 2005. He was a partner in the Toronto office of my firm. We met at a partners' retreat. Where else was a single mother of a one-year-old child supposed to meet anyone?

For a year, Paul and I managed a long-distance relationship. I took my daughter with me on trips to Toronto every other weekend. Eventually, the arrangement became unsustainable. If we were going to build a family life together, someone had to move. I made the decision in 2006. Paul was petrified, but it was time to take that leap, so I did. I made the tough choice to leave my well-established Quebec civil law legal practice, along with my family and friends. I was thirty-six years old. Obviously, I was driven to succeed because I wanted my life with Paul and our blended family to work. He was a devoted father to three boys aged six, nine, and eleven. Uprooting myself was the only way for us to be together.

I didn't have any worries because I trusted that I could make our lives better, richer, and happier. I felt it deep in my gut. On the contrary, Paul was considerably worried about my career, the drastic changes to my life, and the potential impact of failure on our relationship. He didn't want to be the reason I gave up everything I'd built professionally up to that point.

Moving to Toronto meant leaving my friends and family behind, as well as going back to school to requalify as a common law lawyer and to write the Ontario Bar exams. I had a thriving career in Quebec, and my daughter was just two years old and didn't speak a word of English. What if it didn't work out? That was Paul's fear, but I knew it would.

There was no self-doubt this time. I took the reins and seized control, following my instincts because the path was clear. Paul had three young sons, and I had always wanted a larger family of my own. Being adopted instilled that deep desire. Before Florence was born, I'd had three miscarriages, which led me to believe I wouldn't have another child. I wanted my daughter to have siblings, and I was deeply in love with Paul. He was the love of my life, and I adored his sons.

I had one goal, and it was to create a family with him. Everything was going so well between us and the kids. It felt like everything I wanted was sitting right there on a silver platter. I was making another choice to control my destiny. I was going to move, and I was going to make it work. There was a bigger picture and a larger dream here than just my career.

The first step I took was to speak to my firm. I went to the chair of the litigation department and explained what I wanted to do. I asked, I had a plan, and I knew how it could work. Despite the firm's support to ensure a smooth transition to the Toronto office, the move still turned out to be a far greater cultural shock than I anticipated.

It took eighteen months of brutal work to get requalified as a common law lawyer. Between studying and taking exams, I was still practicing law full time between Montreal and Toronto and, on some days, minding four children under the age of twelve at home. My family and friends thought I was crazy. It was insane, but I kept my eyes on the prize.

The next important step was to take control of my career in this new market, where I was essentially unknown. It was 1993 all over again. I had to rebuild my professional network from scratch. Once again, I made a deliberate decision to be everywhere—attend every conference and every cocktail event. I did everything I could to rebuild my network, only this time I had children at home and a busy family life. Time management became crucial.

I got involved with various organizations in the legal profession, such as the Advocates Society, initially as a skills instructor, and eventually taking on leadership roles. My involvement helped me connect with members of the Ontario Bar and Bench. It was, and continues to be, an amazing way to build and nurture a network, while also making friends. The Society provided a treasure trove of camaraderie among colleagues.

I also recognized an opportunity in my field of defense class action work. There was no class action section at the Ontario Bar Association (OBA), and I saw an urgent need for one. I found the name of the executive director and made my pitch, outlining the need for such a class action section. It took a while, but it finally got approved. Again, I asked, I had a plan, and I had the ability to carry it through.

I created the section in 2008 and recruited lawyers from the plaintiff and defense bars to sit on the executive committee. Together, we established an annual class action conference, and the first OBA Class Action Colloquium was held the same year. In 2023, it celebrated its 15th anniversary. The section still exists and is now thriving under the next generation's leadership.

That vision and decision allowed me to get to know several members of the Ontario Class Action Bar and Bench, and to develop long-lasting friendships. It was an important step in rebuilding my network in a province where I was essentially unknown just two years prior. Had it not been from my involvement with the Advocates Society and the OBA, I wouldn't have felt so comfortable taking control over my own destiny in a new legal market so quickly.

A similar event followed with the creation of the Canadian Bar Association's (CBA) Task Force on National and Multijurisdictional Class Actions. Following the adoption of class action legislation in multiple provinces, it became apparent that we were running into a massive problem—overlapping cases with a total lack of coordination. Waiting for legislative amendments to address some of the issues would take too long, so I went to the CBA and explained why I thought we needed a national task force to tackle the problem.

I gathered support and interest before launching what would become more than a ten-year endeavor. I took it on and proposed we establish a task force composed of lawyers from each province with class action legislation, from both sides of the aisle, as well as members of the judiciary. The CBA agreed to the project, and I became the chair of this task force. What better way to build a network across the country? It allowed me to get to know the entire class action Bar and Bench nationally.

I saw an opportunity—a gap that needed to be filled—and I knew I could lead this project. The judicial protocol the task force eventually drafted was incorporated into the practice directions of most provinces and the Federal Court. While the motivation behind creating this task force was solving a genuine problem rather than personal gain, there's no doubt I benefited from the networking opportunities it provided. It certainly launched my career outside of Quebec.

It's crucial to put fear aside and summon the courage to ask. Just ask. You won't get anything if you don't. Years ago, when I wanted to become a member of the International Association of Defense Counsel, I had to seek a sponsor, as membership requires an invitation. I was still new to Toronto and no one at my firm was a member, so they couldn't nominate me. However, thanks to my networking, I had many friends practicing at other Toronto firms. A partner at a competing firm was a member, so I asked if he'd nominate me. Just like that. And he did. By a competitor, nonetheless. I asked.

Fear often deters people from asking. Just ask. The worst they can say is no. Consider the alternative: what if they say yes?

This reminds me of a line by poet Erin Hanson:

> *"What if I fall?"*
> *Oh, but my darling,*
> *What if you fly?*

In other words, trust yourself and jump.

That philosophy also led me to leave what had been my home for twenty-three years. By 2013, Ogilvy Renault/Norton Rose Fulbright had been the longest relationship of my life. My decision to join Torys was closely tied to the importance of stepping outside my comfort zone and taking control of my destiny, despite the risks and fear of failure.

It was about recognizing and seizing a golden opportunity when it presented itself. Joining Torys in February 2013 and opening its Montreal office was a crucial decision in leaving what had become a stale environment and pursuing happiness and fulfillment in my professional life.

While the decision to leave Montreal was driven by my love for Paul, it ultimately led to a much more fulfilling career with a broader scope and greater opportunities, including joining Torys. The choice had a positive domino effect on my professional life. Everything happens for a reason. Was it easy? Absolutely not. It took dedication and an enormous amount of work, but it remained within my control. In my hands.

In 2023, I received the OBA Class Action Lawyer of the Year award. While I had received many accolades before, that one meant a lot to me because it was a recognition by my peers in Toronto—a place where many thought I would never truly make it.

Reading the reference letters supporting my nomination, including one from an opposing counsel and another from the former Chief Justice of

Ontario, made me realize the fear Paul and I had that I wouldn't succeed in Toronto were unfounded. I'd made it. In spades.

Would I have succeeded without taking all those initiatives? I'll never know, but being the master of my own destiny has served me quite well. I didn't wait. And I didn't listen to the shoulder devil as it whispered, "You're too young" and "Nobody knows you, so no one will trust you."

Only one person will push my ideas, and that's me. No one can push your ideas forward better than you. You may have champions to help you along the way, and you absolutely need help, but someone needs to drive the show. Yes, it's you. You should be the driver of your own life. If you don't take the wheel, you'll be stuck in the same spot forever.

Being the master of my own destiny also meant staying true to who I am. I kept my destiny in my own hands by embracing my authentic self. While I could have tried to fit into a mold, I chose to make it work for me as I was. If I had tried the whole "fake it until you make it" thing, it wouldn't have worked.

That's the strength of being the master of your destiny. Pretending to be somebody else doesn't make you as strong of a person. Confidence in the choices you make plays a significant role in shaping your destiny.

I want to stress how making choices and taking control of your life is deeply connected to not losing yourself in the chaos of what you're trying to control or accomplish. We often take care of everyone around us and neglect our own needs. This is especially prevalent among women. I learned this lesson the hard way, and it nearly broke me. But I survived, and it led to my second rebirth.

In 2023 and the early part of 2024, I dealt with a few crises at the same time. They served as a harsh wake-up call that highlighted my need to set boundaries, as I was drowning. For the first time in my life, I broke, surprising everyone who knew me and believed I was unbreakable. I shattered the Superwoman myth.

First, my father was diagnosed with vascular dementia. He often left his apartment, unable to remember where he was, wandered outside in winter wearing slippers, and frequently experienced aggressive outbursts. At the same time, my mother was battling bladder cancer. Having gone almost fully deaf and legally blind, she couldn't take care of him. It was one crisis after another the entire year—my dad's confusion, the constant crying, the daily stress, and the guilt.

My siblings and I had to separate our parents by placing my dad in a specialized nursing home.

This decision significantly increased my financial burden, given that I was the sole payer of their living expenses, which had now more than tripled. More importantly, my sister Sophie and I found ourselves on the front lines. We were the receivers of my dad's crisis calls, the organizers of medical appointments for both parents, tending to their daily needs, and holding down the fort 24/7, over and above managing our own careers and family responsibilities.

For months, taking care of our dad during his transition was essentially a full-time job. I also faced conflicts with my mother, which brought me right back to the environment I had left at sixteen years old. It was an incredibly draining period, both physically and emotionally.

Second, despite my law firm being a loving and happy place to work with supportive colleagues, by the end of January 2024, I was running on adrenaline. After thirty-one years of practice, I was working two to three times more than ever before. The Montreal office was thriving, as was the national class action practice. We became the victims of our own success. Too many files too many clients. I simply had way too much on my plate, and it was not sustainable.

Third, and *le coup de grâce*, was a complete breakdown in communication with my twenty-year-old daughter, with whom I was very close. By then, I had no fuel left in the tank to navigate this last crisis. It broke me and brought me to my knees. For the first time in my life, I felt utterly disoriented and completely broken. I couldn't function, sleep, work, wash, or eat. For days, I was unrecognizable. My husband was extremely worried.

Everything had piled up, and I wanted to throw in the towel. I said, "That's it. I'm fed up with being the rock for everybody." Everyone in my life pulled me in every single direction. I was tired of being strong for everybody else—the person everybody goes to. So, I collapsed. For someone like me, admitting defeat was a big deal, but I had reached that point.

I was saying to myself, "I'm done. I'm done. Finished. I don't want to do that anymore." I attended therapy, and with the support of the firm, my partners, and Paul, I took some time off for myself. I needed to recharge. To reset. I took a six-week hard stop—a complete disconnection for the first time in my career. No calls. No emails. Just me, myself, and I. That was a conscious decision I made because it had to happen. It didn't mean I didn't feel guilty. I did. I was abandoning ship, which wasn't at all in my nature.

It was long overdue. I should have done it sooner. My desire to control my destiny had gone a little too far, and I'd forgotten about my health in the process. No one can be in control all the time. Everyone needs to learn how to let go. It took an accumulation of crises for me to recognize that being in control also meant knowing when to say no and taking time for myself.

It was right around that time when I was asked to author this book. I received an email from the publisher, and I told my husband, "This is ridiculous. Why now? Who am I going to motivate?"

I was at the lowest point in my life, aside from when I had the miscarriages. I was in no position to motivate anybody. My husband said I'd bounce back and have another story to tell.

I ignored the request and left for Italy—my happy place—where we have a vacation home and many friends. It's where I recharge and reconnect. On the advice of my therapist, I surrounded myself with beauty, art, and nature to reflect and recharge.

A good friend of mine in Siena, Federica—my "spiritual sister"—organized a special dinner for me in the middle of a mountain, in an isolated little hut with an extraordinary chef. She called that day my "renaissance" because this trip was going to be my rebirth. Indeed, it was.

When I came back from Italy, I patched things up with my daughter, which was key to my recovery. Then, for the first time in my life, I set some strict boundaries with everybody, both personally and professionally. I had no boundaries before. I never said no to anyone . . . ever.

I'm extremely generous and would put myself in debt to give money to other people. I used to deprive myself of sleep and exercise to give time to others. I'd never put myself first before. Never, ever, ever. Even after working a twenty-hours day, if someone needed help, I would jump in to help. Always.

It was time to change that, so I took back control of my destiny. I thought of what would help me and proposed a professional development plan to my firm. Of course, they were supportive and implemented the plan. It's been tremendously useful in finding work/life balance and not feeling as if the world would end if I wasn't there.

On the home front, I told my siblings I wasn't going back to doing everything for our parents—

we would share the responsibilities. My youngest sister was already pulling more than her weight, managing three kids and running her own business, but everyone needed to chip in, and most stepped up.

I also set firm boundaries with my daughter. I cut the cord. No one was accustomed to hearing me say, "No." Everyone had to learn to live with the new version of me—the one who puts herself first. The one who occasionally says, "No," and who won't drop everything to help if it's not urgent.

The hardest thing was saying no to my daughter because I'd never done that before. She had to adjust. And she did. Everyone did.

This episode in my life, as difficult as it was, felt like a graduation into mastering my destiny. I was taking back control and letting my natural generosity be repressed to protect myself and prioritize my own needs. This was the message I gave everybody.

For over fifty years, I put everybody else first. That's over. I come first now. This decision to make and keep boundaries is the culmination of reclaiming my destiny. If I hadn't done it, I never would have returned to my wonderful career and colleagues, and I probably wouldn't have reconnected with my family. Being the master of my life has given me a new life. I could have gotten really sick, but I seized control, and it took only six weeks.

The biggest challenge was to actually execute my new plan and uphold those boundaries. Funnily, sometimes my daughter would fall back on her old habits and expect immediate help with trivial things, and I'd have to remind her that the old mom was gone, and that the new mom was on her own schedule. I no longer took ownership of others' responsibilities. Each person in my life now carries their own weight.

My advice for people who give their all for everyone else is to learn how to prioritize yourself. As you take care of others, make sure you're on that list too. Make a conscious decision to not leave yourself behind. Don't react to everything in your life, or all the things that can pull you in every direction. You can lose years this way. So, remember—you are the master of your life. The quality of your life. The success of your life. It's all in your hands. Your life is just as important as anyone else's. It's actually the most important.

Successful women often take on too much, assuming the role of caretaker for everyone in their life. As Author Lysa TerKeurst puts it, boundaries are "the skin between survival and surrenders . . .

they are how you say: This far, and no further." This perfectly captures what I went through in 2024.

I took control again. I made the decision. I hold my boundaries. And I'm so much better for it. The next half of my life—of my destiny—is completely mine. I'm the driver once more, and I'm not going off the road again.

3

HAVE THE COURAGE TO STEP OUTSIDE YOUR COMFORT ZONE

Stepping outside my comfort zone has never come naturally. The unknown has always made me uneasy, often to the point of feeling physically sick. Perhaps this discomfort stems from not knowing where I came from. For a long time, I had no anchor or sense of stability. Being uprooted so often instilled in me a deep fear of the unknown: "What will happen next?"

Fear is a powerful thing. Many people become completely paralyzed by it, depriving themselves of truly living. I chose a different path. I pushed through my fears, and you can too.

For a long time, my way of managing fear was to be in constant control by looking ahead and planning my next steps. Obviously, this ties into wanting to be the master of my own destiny. I am the ultimate planner. Going with the flow is not something I do well. By planning everything, I thought I wouldn't have to be afraid, as I would know exactly what would happen next, and I didn't have to feel insecure about it.

This is quite odd for a litigator, given how unpredictable a courtroom is. Somehow, I overcame that dichotomy in my career. Although, I still over prepare for everything and try to anticipate every angle, but that's the staple of being a good advocate. My insecurities about the unknown and my need for control turned out to be assets as a lawyer.

Strangely, my fear of the unknown has never prevented me from jumping and doing what needs to be done, no matter how uncomfortable it makes me feel. Remember that fear in the change room at the Quebec Games? How did I use stress as fuel? I did the same with my fear of the unknown. Clearly, I have stepped outside my comfort zone and ventured into the unknown on multiple occasions since the beginning of my career—probably more than most people. Each time, despite the fear, it was for the better. I moved forward. I grew. But was it ever stressful and scary each time!

From the age of five, venturing beyond my comfort zone triggered physical reactions. I recall waiting for the bus to go to kindergarten and having knots in my stomach, cramps, and diarrhea. The fear of doing something I'd never done before made me sick. It was very scary.

Like that first bus ride, the same happened when I started high school. The week before school started, I had to go see where I was going. To familiarize myself with the routine, I rode the bus, walked the route, went down the corridors, and found my locker. I went to each classroom so I knew where they were and how to get from one to the next. Preparing for the change and planning each moment of my day made it feel less daunting. I could visualize my new environment, and that comforted me.

Not much had changed by the time I started law school. I was from a small town, so for me, Montreal was the big city. Just getting to the school building was a daunting venture. I had never set foot in the subway. I'm actually embarrassed to tell this story—I was nineteen years old, and right up to the first day of class, I still had to rehearse the whole route. There was no way I could just go with the flow. I wouldn't have been able to handle just getting up and winging it on the first day of class. I needed to be comfortable with where I was going, and know how I was going to get there and what to expect.

I've gotten better with age, but I still trust in planning. Prepare, practice, and plan. To feel comfortable, I need to know what will happen tomorrow.

When I started my career as a lawyer, I was nervous, but it didn't feel like I was stepping outside my comfort zone. I was clearly in my element because I really wanted to be a lawyer. It's like an actor experiencing performance anxiety before stepping on stage, except I was entering a courtroom. Over thirty years later, I still get butterflies, but I've never felt uncomfortable or physically sick because I was doing what I wanted to do. I feel most at home in a courtroom. In fact, taking the subway for the first time was more nerve-wracking than stepping into a courtroom for the first time. This experience illustrates that comfort zones aren't always logical. They have nothing to do with the importance of the task or the goal at hand.

While courtrooms have never scared me, practicing law in a non-native language did. At twenty-three years old, I barely spoke English. I was advised that I needed to significantly improve my English to be successful at the firm, given our client base. Rather than shying away from this learning opportunity, I intentionally chose files that involved Anglophone clients so I could improve my English. It was intensely uncomfortable, and it would have been easier to cherry pick Francophone cases, where I would have excelled.

Of course, I didn't want to fail, so I had to work a lot harder to ensure my work was perfect. I was deliberately stepping outside my comfort zone to reach the next level. Planning what I wanted to accomplish required me to move beyond what would have been within my comfort zone.

The thing about comfort zones is that they can be reassuring. They provide a stabilizing, warm, safe, and fuzzy place to be. Many people stay in their zone and are happy doing so. However, for those who seek change and growth, it rarely happens without stepping outside of that zone. You won't learn if you remain in your safe place. You must push beyond it and do things you've never done before.

Along the way, you'll make mistakes, but you'll learn how to work more efficiently and effectively to minimize those mistakes and become better at whatever it is you're leaning. There is no other way. Success is not a standstill thing; it's a constant process that involves continually learning, changing, and growing.

More often than not, things happen for a reason. Whether you saw it coming or not, an event can force you to change. It pushes you out of your comfort zone so you can rebuild. When I moved with Paul to Ontario, I had been practicing law in Montreal for thirteen years and had already made partner. Moving to another city was extremely uncomfortable. I didn't have any friends, family, or professional connections in Toronto. The move was essentially a deep dive into the great unknown.

Compared to Toronto, Montreal is a small city. Even the commute between our home in the suburbs and my downtown office proved to be a challenge. So many people! Just like I'd done in high school and university, I had to learn the route before my first day. It was uncomfortable and overwhelming, which seems ridiculous, really. Looking back, it sounds completely silly, but this illustrates how deeply afraid I am of anything unfamiliar.

The Montreal office of Ogilvy Renault had been my home since I was twenty years old. I knew every corner and could even point out a new crack in the wall. I grew up there. When I first walked into the Toronto office, it felt strange. I didn't know many people, nor did I know my way around. Stepping into a Toronto courtroom was strange too. The judges there didn't know me. In a way, I felt like I was starting my career all over again.

Meeting Paul, moving to Toronto to start a family life together, and getting requalified as a common law lawyer all presented challenges. The journey was plagued with roadblocks and uncomfortable moments, but it also created incredible opportunities.

Although I was supposed to leave my Quebec civil law practice behind and transition to full-time common law practice in the Toronto office, I ended up creating a rather unique career for myself—one that led to my fulfilling and successful career with Torys practicing law across the country with my dual civil-common law calls to the Bar opened doors that would not have been available to me had I stayed in Montreal. I developed a nationwide legal practice that ultimately gave me an edge on the legal market.

What some thought would be career suicide became the reason for my success. I created my own niche, all because I fell in love with Paul and moved to Toronto to find happiness in my personal life. My choices became the core reason for my professional successes, and that was not planned at all—an unexpected result for someone who plans everything!

I didn't let fear paralyze me. From an academic standpoint, the requalification process took eighteen months, but the feeling of "I've finally made it on Bay Street" took about two years. Two years!

It didn't just fall from the sky; it took two years of hustling and working hard, just as it did back when I was a young lawyer in Montreal and nobody knew me. I got out there and I got involved. I helped myself.

Despite putting all that effort in, it was still two years before I could say to Paul, "I went to a cocktail today. I walked into the room, and for the first time, I felt like I was back in Quebec because I could navigate the crowd comfortably."

I prepared, planned, got involved, learned, and made mistakes. That's what helped me get through all those times of intense fear and discomfort. I would never claim that, just because I'm an intelligent lawyer, I don't find it difficult to overcome fear and discomfort. This is a fallacy—an illusion people have when they see someone successful. It doesn't mean they don't face their challenges or that they're keeping to their comfort zones, not bothering to push through.

You have to change and get used to feeling uncomfortable for a while. Put in the hard work until you do, and you will feel comfortable again. But by moving from point A to point B, you've progressed. Success is a series of progressions, one after another. The act of hustling is actually comforting to me, and maybe that's my fuel to push through.

I needed to do what it took to eliminate the discomfort, which meant repeating what I'd done in Montreal. My motivation was to eliminate my discomfort. I wanted to find that comfort zone within my profession, where interacting with my network and colleagues felt familiar and natural. My common law qualification didn't provide the same ease and confidence I felt with my civil law training. Getting there took work. It always takes work.

I recall my first hearing in Toronto. I wasn't nervous about making submissions, but I was nervous about the setting. Do you recall the distinctions in robes lawyers wear in Toronto versus Montreal? The chairs were also different. I was used to a different setup. In Quebec, my opponent was in front of me, not beside me like in Toronto. There was a podium, which we didn't have in Quebec, and it was too high for me. The entire administration of justice was different. In Montreal, there's one courthouse. In Toronto, there are many.

Just like in high school, I had to go see the place the day before. I remember arriving extremely early before the first court hearing because I was uncomfortable with the physical setup—not with what I was going to say, but with the unfamiliar environment.

Once I started my submissions, I was in my element. I got so comfortable that, after a few hours on my feet and without realizing it, I switched to speaking French mid-sentence. I said, "Please take *onglet 11 de mon cahier d'autorités*", which means "tab eleven of my book of authorities." The judge smiled and asked if I'd continue in English so he could follow. This absent-minded switch to my native tongue was a clear indicator that I felt at home.

I didn't have a transition period when I moved from Montreal to Toronto. The moment I arrived, I was thrust into the lion's den. At first, I tried to adapt and change my ways to become a "real" Toronto lawyer. My attempt to become someone else to succeed—to mimic what I thought was the right style of advocacy in this new market—only pushed me further outside my comfort zone.

I needed to be comfortable to shine, and while I changed my Quebec courtroom robe for the Ontario one, I quickly reverted to my own style of advocacy—the style that had made me successful in Quebec. My comfort zone.

I'm grateful to the Ontario Bench and Bar for their warm welcome. I realized I couldn't change who I was, nor how the lawyers were in Toronto, or the system itself. Instead, I had to develop a new comfort level to perform at my best. From a professional standpoint, this was difficult. I wanted to give up during the requalification process because I didn't think I was going to make it. Initially, I thought I needed to become a chameleon, emulating Toronto lawyers to feel comfortable; however, I didn't completely change my ways. Certain things stayed the same and probably helped me in the long run. I rebuilt my professional life and eventually became as comfortable in Toronto as I had been in Quebec.

Just as I was feeling comfortable again, a new career opportunity arose when Torys approached me to join them as a partner. The amazing Trisha Jackson was going to retire in ten years or so, and they needed me for the succession of the class action and product liability practice. At that time, I was forty-two years old and had been with Ogilvy Renault/Norton Rose Fulbright for twenty-two years. It was my family and my home, and the only constant in my life since I was twenty. It doesn't get any more comfortable than that.

At first, I declined to even meet with Torys. I had been building this unique nationwide class action practice and splitting my time between Toronto and Montreal. I was thriving. Why on earth would I want to rock the boat and make another change?

Torys didn't even have a Montreal office, and there was no way I'd give up the uniqueness of my dual civil/common law practice. In my opinion, Torys was the ultimate conservative, blue-chip firm, and I figured I was too colorful for them.

Les Viner, the managing partner of Torys at the time, was persistent in pursuing a meeting with me, but I just wasn't interested. Years later, I learned that Linda Plumpton (the lawyer I considered the best Canadian litigator of my generation) had something to do with Mr. Viner not accepting "no" for an answer. She eventually became my friend, my partner, and someone I admire deeply. I am truly grateful she didn't give up on me.

I eventually caved and accepted a meeting with Mr. Viner and the then-lead of the litigation department, Crawford Smith. It was December 2012, a week before the holidays, and I really didn't want to go back downtown for what I thought would be a useless meeting. After Mr. Viner insisted, I told him he would have to drive to the suburbs for a meeting, as I was leaving the next day for Mont-Tremblant, Quebec, where we had rented a cottage for the holiday break. He agreed and drove about an hour west of Toronto.

We had lunch at a restaurant so I could leave if I felt the need to. I was completely closed off. With my arms crossed, I let my body language make it clear that I wasn't interested. Aside from the obvious fact that Torys had no Montreal office, I argued that my current platform was better, etc. I wanted that meeting to end so I could go on vacation with my family. I literally told Mr. Viner, "You're like a first date; you have absolutely no credibility, and you're just telling me everything I want to hear. But I don't believe you."

You see, Mr. Viner was in sell mode. Over and above praising my career, he was also selling me on the culture of the firm. He was right to focus on that, because Torys has a unique culture. I was secretly star-struck that this firm was interested in me, but I sincerely doubted what he was telling me about the firm's culture was true. In the cutthroat and competitive legal market, I didn't expect such a culture to still exist. I had grown up in a similar culture, but over the years, profitability took precedence over other values, and I just assumed it was the same across all large Canadian law firms.

I think they needed to meet with me in person to assess whether I was who they thought I was and if I would fit the firm's culture of collaboration. It's not a culture that suits everyone; however, it resonated with me because it felt like home, reminiscent of my time at Ogilvy Renault in the 1990s and early 2000s.

I still didn't believe what Mr. Viner was telling me, nor did I think I would fit in. From a cultural standpoint, yes, the Torys way was music to my ears, but I still doubted I was talented enough for a firm like Torys.

Although I wasn't interested, Mr. Viner had done a good job in selling the firm's culture because I spent my holidays pondering the points he'd made. In January, I spoke to a couple of trusted senior partners at various firms on Bay Street. They all told me, "No, no! You can't just say no to Torys. Think this one through because it's nothing like the other offers you got in the past."

Something that really stuck with me came from the late Charles Scott, a respected senior litigator in Toronto. Charles started his career as an articling student at Torys with today's most respected and decorated litigator in the country, Sheila Block. He left Torys to open the Toronto office of Ogilvy Renault in the late 1990s, but then started his own litigation boutique firm with a few colleagues of his. I looked up to Charles and often sought his advice. He said, "Sylvie, Torys is the last-standing true partnership on Bay Street. Give this offer some serious thought, because you'd be a fool to ignore it."

That's when I seriously thought about the offer and did my due diligence. The courting period was overwhelming. Torys was very convincing. Meetings were organized with fabulous lawyers, including some female lawyers I had admired all my life: Trisha Jackson, Sheila Block, Linda Plumpton, and Wendy Matheson. These were monuments in my profession. They wanted me, for which I was flattered. They definitely showed me the love when they said the firm would open a Montreal office, allowing me to pursue my national practice and build a team there. The whole thing kept me up at night. I was confused, anxious, and excited. Still, I wasn't ready.

It wasn't about money. Other firms had offered me significantly higher-paying positions, but none ever interested me. I didn't want to leave what I considered my home—my happy place. And I certainly didn't want to face another change just six years after the move to Toronto. I didn't see the need to put myself in an uncomfortable zone again and preferred to stay in my comfort zone. I always thought I would retire from Ogilvy Renault and never go anywhere else.

It took a little kick in the butt to force me to decide—a kick I gave myself in February 2013 following an incident with a partner at my prior firm, which was sort of the last straw from a cultural standpoint. In an instant, I saw what the next twenty years of my career might look like if I stayed, and I said to myself, "That's it, I'm done." I picked up the phone, called Mr. Viner, and I said, "Okay, I'm coming."

It turned out that everything about Torys was true. The culture was a perfect fit for me. The meeting with Mr. Viner wasn't just a sales pitch, but the firm's reality. In the twelve years I've been with Torys, I've been incredibly happy. Although I still feel undeserving of being asked to step into Trisha Jackson's shoes (truthfully, no one can fill those shoes!), leading Torys's national class action and product liability practice groups has been a genuine honor.

The team comprises the best of the best. My partners are true partners. We support each other and rise and fall together. Because we really, really like each other, we operate like a tight-knit family. Opening and leading the Torys Montreal office has been one of the greatest joys and privileges of my career.

When we opened that office on April 4, 2013, it was just me and my legal assistant, Celine, who had already been with me for eighteen years. She is the definition of loyalty, and also had to step outside her comfort zone to leave Ogilvy Renault after twenty-six years to join me at Torys.

Now, after twelve years, our office has grown to over forty-five legal and non-legal professionals, including six partners without whom I wouldn't have been able to build this successful office. Torys is a well-established player in the Montreal market, and we are still growing. We are truly the dream team.

Aside from having my daughter and marrying Paul, joining Torys was the best decision of my life. Since February 2013, I haven't regretted summoning the courage to make that move. I thought I was happy at my previous firm, and I was for many years; however, somewhere along the way, I grew resigned to my situation, settling for what I believed was unavoidable in the legal market. My desire to remain comfortable blinded me to other opportunities. Joining Torys was truly a transformative decision—one I almost missed out on because I hesitated to step outside my comfort zone.

Everything happens for a reason. My decision to move to Toronto, although grounded in personal motivations, gave me a unique professional edge. I would have never built that distinctive dual civil/common law national practice if I hadn't moved to Toronto, and I doubt Torys would have considered me for succession planning had I been based solely in Montreal. The professional awards I received, the various fabulous board positions I secured, and my distinctive career trajectory all stemmed from deciding to follow my heart and be with Paul in Toronto.

Everything snowballed from conscious and difficult decisions I made in the past. I left three relationships, throwing myself out of my comfort zone each time because I needed more from my partnerships to feel supported and aligned. I needed to be challenged more often in my professional career. Although I suffered from bouts of fear of the unknown, along with physical symptoms and the sense that the odds were against me, I still pushed through. There were days, weeks, and months of perpetual discomfort, but I accepted it as part of the process. I worked hard to get back into the groove of a new practice, a new legal system, and working with new colleagues. Ultimately, it all paid off. Being uncomfortable does pay off.

This also applied to my personal life. I had to work hard and put in the effort to create the family life I wanted; however, I was very much outside my comfort zone by taking on three young stepsons in addition to my toddler, all while juggling my professional responsibilities. The need to adapt was significant for all six of us. My two-year-old daughter only spoke French when we moved in with Paul and the boys, and they only spoke English. I recall the dinner table exchanges with questions like, "What did she say?" and *"Qu'est-ce qu'ils ont dit?"* The boys would correct my English if I mispronounced words because I used to put an 'h' in front of everything. For instance, I would say "h'oven," and the boys would say, "No, it's o-ven." It became a running joke.

Family life, while different, was also a lot of fun. I was grateful that everyone chipped in to help me improve my English, and thanks to her stepbrothers, my daughter was fluent in English within six months. Overall, we were fortunate. Merging families can be difficult, but we didn't have any major roadblocks. Paul and I shared similar parenting styles. I never heard, "You're not my mother," from the boys. They still had their mother, and I was not trying to replace her. Paul could be a full-time father to my daughter, as her biological father was still living in Mexico, and we remained good friends. Diego had no such insecurities about this dynamic—a rare trait—and he was grateful that Florence had Paul in her life.

It took a lot of effort to coordinate our schedules to accommodate everyone's obligations and activities. I was no longer the one fully in control of the schedule, which required me to learn how to let go. I could no longer control everything, which was a challenge. I had to adapt to last-minute changes and unexpected events. This is all part of the experience of having a blended family and a busy life.

It was very different and required more work than just being alone with my daughter, but it was also the family life I wanted. We all had to juggle our responsibilities, but I didn't feel uncomfortable with this new family dynamic. I simply had to adapt to the new challenges I was facing. Of course, there was a lot more noise in the house with young boys jumping on couches, slamming doors, as boys do. It created a different vibe compared to being alone with a baby girl.

Fortunately, there was no competition among the kids. Because Florence was so young, the three boys practically treated her like a little doll. I have a great picture of the boys on the couch and my little daughter on top of them, wearing her diaper and holding her bottle of milk. It's one of my favorite pictures of the kids, and it was their first weekend spending time together. In hindsight, I can honestly say it went very well from the start. They have enriched our lives, and it has been so much better for my daughter. Florence is more well-rounded because of the male influence in her life, and she's definitely tougher.

She has a great life, with friends and family in Quebec and Ontario. She's also trilingual, speaking French, English, and Spanish, and has a developed a competitive sports career that she may not have had if we'd stayed in Montreal. Her activities include Irish dancing, eventing, and boxing with Olympian Mandy Bujold.

Not only is her family life much more fun with three stepbrothers, she also has an extended family on her biological father's side in Puerto Vallarta, including half siblings, and cousins, whom she visits regularly. She will finish her undergraduate degree at the University of Western Ontario in 2026, and have a bright future ahead of her.

Stepping outside my comfort zone has also brought me joy and happiness, and created opportunities for fresh adventures in my personal life that I never would have experienced had I chosen to "stay in my lane." This includes my passion for horses. Given my circumstances growing up, I obviously had no experience with these magnificent animals. I had a cat, and that was it.

When my daughter was five, we lived in an area with equestrian farms all around us. Florence asked to take riding lessons after attending a summer camp in our neighbourhood. As I took her to lessons each week and helped her groom and tack her pony, I fell in love with the horses at the stable. It brought me peace and balance, much like the lake in North Hatley did when I had the cottage before moving to Ontario to be with Paul. What started as a once-a-week hobby became a passion for breeding. I bought my first horse at an auction and started riding for the first time at thirty-nine years old.

After a few months of lessons, my horse was getting fat, and we discovered she was pregnant! Thus, the adventure began—night checks or sleeping at the barn to not miss the baby's birth and learning horsemanship on the fly. It was unbelievably rewarding. I had support, of course, and I was eager to learn.

Soon, I had another horse, and then another one. At one point, I owned eleven horses. I was getting attached to the foals and couldn't bring myself to sell them. Each separation felt like reliving my adoption. Hearing the mare scream for her baby was heart breaking.

I drew immense joy and pleasure from the process alongside my friend Tessa, who owned the barn. I learned everything from finding the stallion, inseminating, performing ultrasounds, and handling births—which we without a veterinary present—to nursing foals and picking up the placenta for the veterinary to inspect the next day. We even dealt with twins. I had to learn what to do if the foal was presenting the wrong way, how to break the bag, and cut the cord, etc. On weekends at the barn, I was worlds away from the legal world!

I loved watching the babies grow. Seeing them trained, broken, and ridden for the first time was outside my comfort zone, but it was so much fun. My daughter competed, and I was riding regularly in dressage. Some of my babies became extraordinary champions in dressage, show jumping, and even eventing after we moved to my friend Judith's barn to try a different aspect of the sport. I became a show horse mom, driving them around for competitions and sponsoring young riders. Watching them succeed was thrilling.

Paul built a barn at home for me so I could bring two of my horses home every weekend. Just sitting and watching them graze produced the same effect as massage—peace and relaxation. I learned to drive a horse trailer. Backing that thing up was petrifying, but I did it. I cleaned stalls, fed horses, and everything in between. The lawyer in me vanished on weekends. I was a horsewoman at heart. There really is nothing more relaxing than shovelling manure.

With these experiences came painful heartache too. There were so many hospitalizations, I could have earned an honorary veterinary degree after dealing with the various medical conditions my horses had over the years. I lost one horse to botulism, a type of food poisoning caused by botulinum bacterium. I watched as he passed away at the peak of his life. My heart broke more than once, but my love for horses made it all worth it. It was the same with my three golden retrievers. Losing two of them in the same year was devastating, but what these animals have brought to my life is priceless. Animals are magical—they see through your soul, comfort you, and know when you're happy or sad. They are my drug, my dopamine.

And yet, I had to make difficult decisions to grow. Once Paul and I developed a passion for Italy and built another life in a Tuscany, it became difficult to keep the horses. I no longer had time to pursue the passion that taught me patience and brought me joy for over fifteen years.

My friend Tessa accepted to care for my babies, for which I am eternally grateful. I can still see them when I want, but I no longer shoulder the responsibility of caring for them. I still own Victoria, the very first horse I bought at the auction. She's blind and old, but a constant reminder of what started that adventure. And, of course, I still have dogs.

As I embark on a new adventure on our farm in Italy, with vineyards and olive groves, I'll need to learn about a whole new world. My life's richness comes from constantly discovering and pursuing new passions in unfamiliar fields. Too many people don't venture outside of what they know, depriving themselves of great adventures. This is coming from someone who needs to plan and be in control. It seems completely out of character, doesn't it?

It is, and that's the beauty of it. When you push yourself outside that comfort zone, you'll discover a world full of wonders. For career women, with or without children, there's often a blockage with the thought, "I couldn't possibly make time to pursue personal passions on the side." Wrong! You can, and you will. Do not underestimate the importance of incorporating personal passions. I live an incredibly busy life and I still devote some of my free time to the horses, and now to my Italian dream.

Balance is everything, but staying in your comfort zone won't bring you that sense of fulfilment. Find a passion and go for it. Make the time for it.

Sometimes I wonder what would have happened if I had stayed in Montreal. I'd probably still have a successful career at Ogilvy Renault (Norton

Rose Fulbright), remaining a civil law lawyer with a practice similar to hundreds of others around me who found success practicing in Montreal. However, I wouldn't have developed that uniqueness that sets me apart on a national level.

While I would have been close to my family and friends, I wouldn't have had four children at home. From a personal standpoint, I would not have enriched my life or my daughter's life. I'm sure I would have been happy, but not to the extent I have reached by having the courage to make a change, despite all the roadblocks I faced.

My success came from stepping outside my comfort zone. If I had maintained the status quo, my life would have remained the same. Change is possible only by throwing yourself into something new. Uncertainty can be destabilizing, and there's a risk to any decision you make, but you can overcome this. Do not let fear be the limiting force in your life. Challenge yourself. Accept the uncomfortable feeling. Understand the process. And jump.

PRACTICAL TAKEAWAYS

Write down your personal and professional short-term goals (where you want to be in two–three years), and the actions you'll take to achieve them.

_____

_____

Write down your personal and professional medium-term goals (where you want to be in five–seven years), and the actions you'll take to achieve them.

_____

_____

Write down your personal and professional long-term goals (where you want to be in ten–fifteen years), and the actions you'll take to achieve them.

_____

_____

List the things that make you feel like an imposter. What are your triggers? What is your counter message to this?

_____

_____

List the things that make you feel uncomfortable and why. How does this compare to your comfort zone, and what makes that area safe for you?

_____

_____

List one uncomfortable thing you can do per week to practice stepping out of your comfort zone.

_____

_____

4

IGNORE THE WHITE NOISE

Do not believe those who do not believe in you. Many will tell you all the things you cannot do or shouldn't do, but that doesn't make it true. Sometimes they think your goals are unachievable because they couldn't achieve their goals. Some may be envious of you, your drive, or your aspirations, and they'll want to take the wind out of your sails. Others are simply negative, only finding a problem for every solution. And then there are those who are genuinely concerned for you and don't want you to make a huge mistake.

So how do you know whom to believe? Well, you must believe in yourself. The only one who can decide if you can do something or not, is you. Only you know your capabilities, strengths, desires, perseverance, discipline, and dedication. If I had listened to everyone around me, I wouldn't have the life I have. I learned very early on to listen to my intuition. My instincts. That little voice deep inside me has been my guide. Over time, I learned to ignore the "white noise"—the voices and opinions all around me—to focus only on what my gut was telling me. Yes, I've learned to own it.

Negative thoughts not only drown out your positive ones, but also dilute your plans and goals. Many people are incapable of seeing the forest for the trees. The trees represent the white noise from people in your life, but the forest represents your goals.

White noise can take different forms—pessimism, negativity, and perspectives limited by personal beliefs. We all see the world through our own lens, shaped by our own experiences, teachings, families, and culture. What may seem like an impossible hill to climb may not appear so to someone else. The saying "take this with a grain of salt" serves as a precursor to a caveat. Some warnings may very well have merit. When making decisions, especially life-changing ones, it's important to discern which opinions to give weight to and which ones to brush off immediately.

There are those who are genuinely trying to warn you, who are making sure you've checked everything and looked at every angle to avoid making a mistake. That's the good noise. Then there are those who simply don't believe in you, so they'll say, "It's never going to work. You're going to lose. You shouldn't be doing this." That's pessimism and negativity. And then, there are those who are just jealous and will try to bring you down because that would make them feel better about themselves. The white noise coming from the jealous and envious people is, unfortunately, far too prevalent. This is different from pessimism because these folks want you to fail or feel threatened by you in some way. You need to be able to identify these people. It's not that they don't believe in you, it's that they don't want you to succeed. Period.

For me, ignoring the white noise has come naturally since childhood because I have had this innate fire in my belly. I have strong survival instincts, and I am deeply connected to them. I will never completely know where that drive comes from, whether it's in my DNA, the result of being adopted, the urge to be the best, or if it's driven by this deep-seated need to be in control and avoid uncertainties. The bottom line is that I have never really fallen for the white noise. At least, not for long. I've ignored those who told me I couldn't do something my entire life, even when facing constant discouragement.

Having said that, there was a period in my life when the white noise was quite loud, starting with when I was trying to conceive a child. By 2003, at thirty-three years old, I had experienced three miscarriages. The first one was a typical early miscarriage, marked by spotting and non-viable pregnancy, while the other two involved the absence of a heartbeat discovered during the second trimester. By the third miscarriage, I was not in a good state of mind. Still very much pregnant with all the accompanying symptoms, I went into complete denial, believing the doctor was wrong and my baby was still alive. I went to three different private ultrasound clinics, hoping to hear a heartbeat and prove the first doctor wrong. I was losing my mind, refusing to believe the baby inside me was dead. It was very difficult to face the truth.

The doctor attempted to induce labor so I could give birth to my dead baby, thereby avoiding another surgery to remove it. It did not work. That baby did not want to leave my body, which only deepened my denial. The doctor wanted me to carry the baby until I went into labor naturally. My mental state spiralled further. I simply could not believe my child was dead. At some point, I'd had enough, and I begged the doctor to surgically remove it, as I could not function at all.

When I decided to try again a fourth time, my friends and family had a lot of concerns about putting myself through this ordeal again. There was a consensus that I should just stop trying. They suggested adopting or moving on, insisting that pregnancy wasn't for me and that I wasn't getting any younger. White noise.

It's not that I was against adoption. I was just obsessed with the need for a biological connection. I wanted something of my blood. I had a strong maternal instinct, and I absolutely wanted a biological child. I craved a blood-related connection because I didn't have one with anyone. I don't think it's irrational. It obviously stems from my own adoption. I know plenty of families with adopted children who have stronger bonds with their children than those with a biological connection. But in my case, I had convinced myself that there was a void in my life, and I needed that bond. I believed my life would be a failure without a baby I gave birth to.

Then came the counterbalance to the white noise—the amazing Dr. Alice Benjamin, a specialist in high-risk pregnancies at the Royal Victoria Hospital in Montreal. She figured out what the problem was with my prior pregnancies, and because of her, I was able to have my daughter, Florence. Dr. Benjamin was an optimist. She believed, so I believed. Despite the white noise telling me to give up, I persevered. What bolstered my belief and courage to try again was this counterbalance to the white noise. Dr. Benjamin provided me with hope, positivity, and balance. Sometimes, when you're unable to connect with your instincts and feel confused, a counterbalance can be incredibly powerful.

The same thing happened when I decided to move to Toronto in 2006. That was when the white noise around me was the loudest, both professionally and personally. The white noise whispered, "This is career suicide." I was successful and well-respected in Quebec. What did I know about common law? About the Toronto market? The courtrooms? The customs? The practices? People said I wasn't qualified and that I wouldn't fit into the Bay Street "old boys' culture." They claimed I was way too colorful and too French-Canadian to succeed there. People thought I had lost my mind. "I can't believe you're doing this for a guy. Risking your career for love?" They simply didn't believe I could do it, or that I should do it.

Those who truly cared about my happiness and believed in me supported me completely. Many of my senior partners at Ogilvy Renault in Montreal were supportive. They helped me transition, and I focused on those who wanted me to succeed while ignoring the others. I'm grateful to those who trusted me with this life-changing move. They know who they are.

Since my very first interview at Ogilvy Renault, one person in particular deserves a special mention: John Coleman. He saw something in me that may not have been obvious to others. Perhaps it was our common Irish roots, or simply his perceptiveness. He was instrumental in getting me hired as a student at nineteen, and he also witnessed how I fell in love with Paul in 2005. I mean, it literally happened right before his eyes. John was 100 percent behind me when I asked to move my career to Toronto, and his support meant the world to me.

Moving to Toronto to be with Paul and his boys brought concerns from family and friends about undertaking a blended family with four children: "You don't know his kids." "What about your daughter and her future?" "She doesn't even speak English!" "We won't see you anymore." "All your support is here." "You're going to be all alone." "If it doesn't work out, you'll have to come right back, and by then, you'll have destroyed everything you worked so hard to build."

It was reasonable for people to be concerned about me. Merging families is incredibly difficult, and it's not always successful. The move to a new province with a different culture and language was challenging, particularly with my two-yearold daughter, and I wasn't sure if it would work out. If it didn't work out, would I have just gone back? There was a lot of pessimism, but it wasn't directed at Paul, because my family loved him from the beginning. Their concerns were focused on the situation of uprooting myself and merging two families in a different province. They were afraid for me. I think that was the sentiment. People were worried about my decisions. The overall sentiment was that I wasn't thinking straight because I'd been blinded by love and was taking a risk with my daughter and my career.

Other than fearing I was making a mistake, my family was also concerned that I was about to complicate my life unnecessarily. It was pessimistic in a sense. Merging families is difficult, and the challenges were compounded by me traveling back and forth to Montreal while re-qualifying at the Bar. There was a lot of fear and pessimism. To be honest, some of the negative white noise and doubt came from us. The most negative of them all was Paul himself. He was deeply afraid that this was merely an experiment, and that I was going to leave him after a year or two. He feared I would sacrifice too much and ruin my career and life, and then possibly blame him and leave. He didn't want to be the reason for my failure.

But I believed it would work. I knew I was capable of making it work, and I knew what I wanted. I loved Paul. If I had left the decision to him, fear would likely have paralyzed us, and we might never have been together. In 2025, we celebrated twenty years of happiness together. What a shame it would have been to let the white noise interfere with that!

I had to ignore the pessimistic white noise coming from my family and from Paul, who kept asking what would happen if it didn't work out. It was scary for both of us. Your partner's pessimism is hard to ignore. That kind of pressure could have hurt my career, and it would have made Paul feel guilty if something went wrong. I worried about feeling homesick, being transplanted into a completely new life and culture, and the possibility of falling out of love with Paul.

The white noise that enters your life from other people or even from yourself stirs up self-doubt. It can become so loud that it takes over, allowing fear to seep in. Fear is at the base of all negativity, which can paralyze us. It robs us of confidence and belief in what we can do. It can make us give up before we've even tried. I've always wanted to try things, even if failure was a possibility. At least I would know I tried. If I'm wrong, I'm wrong, but if I my gut tells me to go for it, I will.

In my personal life, I chose to focus on those who understood and trusted me to trust my instincts. My sister Sophie, in particular, was my biggest fan. Ignoring the white noise is a lot easier when you have at least one supportive voice in your corner. While it's not always necessary to have that support, it certainly makes things easier when someone encourages you through difficult and unpopular decisions. It balances things out.

Professionally, John and the other partners who supported me were my counterbalance, but I also had a career coach after arriving in Toronto who helped me navigate this new market. She conducted interviews to assess how my peers perceived me, and the responses were, in some way, a collection of white noise. People said things like, "She will never make it if she doesn't tone down her style," and "She's too colorful. She needs to change, otherwise Toronto won't accept her as one of them." That was criticism focused on how I should behave to make it.

If a man has an aggressive style, he's praised for it. But if a woman exhibits that same style, she's labelled as too cocky and aggressive. I was even given the nickname "Pitbull" for a while. Can you imagine a man being called Pitbull because he's aggressive in a professional setting? No, he's usually described as assertive and successful. But I was called Pitbull, which is pejorative, and that was white noise. Thankfully, my career coach told me to do the exact opposite. She said, "Ignore all this white noise and stay true to yourself." So, I eventually did.

Initially, I thought I needed to be like a Toronto lawyer to succeed and forget about what had made me successful in Quebec for thirteen years. Forget my true personality. Big mistake. I tried to control my natural extroverted self, thinking I had to tone it down. Back then, my impression of Toronto litigators was that they were more conservative in court, stoic in front of the podium, and poised. In contrast, I have a more flamboyant and colorful style. I don't stay still behind a podium (which we didn't use in Quebec). I thought I had to change my style to fit in.

For my second Toronto court hearing, I not only wore the new Ontario-style court robe, but also tried to mimic what I thought was the proper

"Toronto style" of advocacy. I was sticking to my written notes, completely ignoring my personal style because I wanted to fit in. It didn't go very well. It lasted about five minutes, because I just couldn't do it. In the end, I decided to be myself. The moment I embraced who I truly am, everything fell into place.

I constantly had to talk to myself to ignore the noise in my head that insisted I fit into a specific mold. All this stemmed from being an outsider. I was a Quebec lawyer, and that was real. When I tried to be like a Toronto lawyer, that was being a fake, which went against my truth and authenticity. It didn't work. Rather, I had to focus on the fact that I had the skills, despite being an outsider. I had to have faith in that. I wasn't an imposter. I was different, and that's not the same thing. I followed my inner voice instead. I'd been successful for thirteen years with that style of mine. So, the market would have to put up with my style. I wasn't going to change my style.

When a partner in the Toronto office of Ogilvy Renault said to me, "I can't put your name in this pitch because you're not a real Toronto lawyer," he was just wrong. I had to keep ignoring that type of white noise. I sensed some jealously from certain individuals who tried to discourage me. Some felt threatened by my ability to practice in both common and civil law, to practice out of the Montreal and Toronto offices, or to have active litigation files in all Canadian provinces. That was a rare combination at the time, and it made me stand out even more as an outsider. Some in Quebec thought I was no longer one of them, while some in Toronto thought I wasn't one of them either. I was an anomaly for a while.

Having reliable and supportive people is important to stay out of the negative mind space white noise can bring to you. I deliberately worked to identify who was on my side. I would go to them to counterbalance, brainstorm, or check in ... or just vent. It's not just about finding those who are going to say yes, yes, yes. It's about those who will speak truthfully and tell you, "Yes, but you need to be careful." People will warn you and test your ideas. Yes-people are not useful. I want my ideas and thoughts to be challenged, but in a healthy way. Guide me away from danger, and root for me against doubt and negativity.

Sometimes white noise and negativity come from within. When Torys was trying to recruit me, there were negative thoughts in my own head—my own creation of white noise. The same thing happened when I opened the Montreal office of Torys. I don't recall anyone telling me, "Are you crazy? The market is saturated. You cannot succeed." There was only support and encouragement, especially from my partners at Torys who all supported the idea without hesitation. Les Viner believed in me and in this idea of opening a Montreal office. The entire partnership did. Did I have doubts? Hesitations? Fear? Of course I did.

By then, I was forty-three years old and had faith in my instincts. This is precisely why Celine was the first person I hired at Ogilvy Renault. She'd been with me pretty much throughout my entire career. I needed her at my side if this was going to work. She had always been my right arm through both successes and defeats. Together, we had gone through a combined seven pregnancies! She knew me inside and out.

I convinced Celine to leave the firm and follow me into the unknown, which was a big jump for her after twenty-seven years at Ogilvy Renault. She trusted me, and for that I am forever grateful. She became the office manager, and as the office grew, I continued to trust my instincts and inner voice while ignoring the white noise. By then, I knew how to size people up and gauge whether they'd fit in or not, and who we needed to make that office a success story. That ability came after years of experience.

Sometimes, ignoring white noise means pushing back against people who tell you that you shouldn't take on a new project—or in my case, a new litigation matter. Such was the case with the Mandy Bujold pro bono matter against the International Olympic Committee (IOC) in 2021. That was the most emotionally difficult, yet most rewarding, case of my career. Many people tried to discourage us from taking that case, saying: "The IOC is too powerful," "No one can challenge them," "This is David and Goliath," and "You will lose." So much white noise.

We were blessed with tremendous emotional and professional counterbalance from the firm and the media because everyone was outraged by the discrimination Mandy faced when the IOC disqualified her from the Tokyo Olympics because she was pregnant or postpartum during the qualification period. We also had the support of many Canadians, as well as the sports world, all of whom were angry about the situation. The cause became more important than the white noise. Someone had to take the case on. We did. And we won. More about that later.

Let me be clear: Ignoring the white noise does not mean burying your head in the sand and refusing to heed sound advice. For younger people just getting started in their careers, while it's important to learn to listen to your inner voice and connect with your instincts, you also all need to follow sage advice. If people are giving me advice, sometimes I take it, but usually only if it's because I agree with it. It takes courage to trust your instincts and inner voice if you disagree with the advice.

That's a different spin on ignoring the white noise. It's not just you. You don't just listen to it, you have to be collaborative and inclusive, and actively listen to people. However, at the end of the day, no organization will work solely on consensus. At some point, someone needs to make a decision.

You've got to find that trusted advisor—that one person you deeply respect and know will be your guiding light. Analyze the pros and cons, because this is not just about doing what you want without thinking. It's about finding the balance between sound advice and white noise. It's about seeing through people, trusting your instincts, and understanding the motivation behind the advice. Ultimately, it's about owning the decision. Only you can determine if it's the right one.

The ability to trust your instincts also comes in handy when you're in a leadership position, because there will always be pessimists who say, "Don't do that . . . We shouldn't do this . . . We shouldn't do that." To be a leader—which is much more than just managing people—you have to follow your inner voice and instincts, otherwise very little is going to move forward. If you allow every disagreement to hinder progress, then growth and development become impossible. Someone needs to make the difficult decisions.

Women probably experience this white noise a lot more than men—the voices whispering, "You can't do this... you can't do that..." or "You shouldn't do this... you shouldn't do that." Step one is recognizing that you have an inner voice. It's there; it exists. With young girls—my daughter, for example—when she's about to make a decision, I always remind her that there's a devil and an angel on each shoulder, and she needs to decide which voice to listen to.

It's interesting that both she and I are bad at multiple-choice tests. How often have you second-guessed your first choice, changed your answer, only to find out you were right the first time? That's your inner voice at work. We tend to constantly question our instincts instead of paying more attention to them.

Of course, you don't just keep your instincts to yourself. Run your intuitions by your champions and mentors to make sure they're valid. I almost never act on difficult decisions without bouncing my intuition off my trusted advisors. Through this exercise, you'll come to understand when your instincts are accurate and when they're not, which will help you build confidence. Eventually, you'll instinctively know you're more often right than wrong.

I'm not always right. I make mistakes. My instincts have led me to believe some past hires would be good fits, but they weren't. The same goes with legal arguments. I love having debates with my team, which is a good way of bouncing my inner voice off them. They will sometimes say, "Oh no, that won't work." And I'll respond, "I don't know, I think it will." And we'll try it. Sometimes I'm right, sometimes I'm not, but that's what keeps me balanced.

I have a few main advisors in my life, some of whom are younger than me, so it's not an age or seniority thing; I've simply identified their talents. Paul is obviously one of them. The others I call "the wise women." My partner Linda is one of them, my friend Lorraine is another, and so is my sister, Sophie. They always provide the right balance of feedback, asking, "Did you think of this? Did you think of that? Do you think this could work?"

Sometimes I feel like I'm always calling them with yet another problem. You have to fight the feeling that you're bothering people or that you're high maintenance. I still do this even though I'm in a leadership position. I trust my inner voice, but I never act on it without bouncing it off somebody else. This is not white noise. This is good noise. Useful noise.

Finally, don't confuse ignoring white noise and remaining authentic with failing to adapt to new cultures, customs, or practices. As mentioned, I did buy the Toronto-style courtroom robe because I was advised to dress the part. That noise came from a well-intended female colleague who was truly trying to help me understand Toronto customs and practices. It's important to understand this. Staying true to yourself doesn't mean being blind to customs and practices. It's like visiting another country, where you have to adapt to their culture. The same thing applies to your professional or personal life, because being stubborn won't help. The mindset of "this is who I am; it's my way or the highway" does not work. Being authentic means not trying to fit in at the expense of what you know you should be or do.

You know what's going to work and what will lead to success. Trying to be someone you're not just isn't going to work. That's a universal truth, no matter what the profession. There's a fine balance between having to be very aware of your surroundings and environment and not completely changing into someone you think others want you to be. That's when you start doubting yourself.

White noise will always be around you. It's up to you not to be led by it, but to use it as guidance. Learn to differentiate between those who don't believe in you, those who want you to fail out of jealousy, and those who are truly concerned and may have valid reasons to be. Stay connected to your instincts. That voice will get stronger and stronger with experience. Next, find your group—your trusted advisors with whom you can bounce off your ideas and plans to make sure they're sound and that you haven't missed anything. This should remain your process no matter how successful you become. This is precisely why having champions and mentors in your life is essential.

5

THE IMPORTANCE OF CHAMPIONS AND MENTORS

Champions and mentors are important to have, both in your professional and personal life, and not just in the early years of your career or as a young adult. I have greatly benefited from having both throughout my life. Too many people underestimate how helpful these folks can be at every stage of life and often confuse the two concepts. Having a champion and a mentor is not the same.

In most businesses or professional environments, there is usually a structure, policy, or process surrounding mentorship. Mentors are typically assigned to us when we start a new position, especially early in our careers. If one isn't assigned, we tend to choose someone with whom we feel comfortable seeking advice—someone to talk to.

It's vital to have a mentor, which is a well-known and proven concept.

A mentor is there to show you the ropes, guide you, and help you learn from mistakes so you can improve in your field. Their role is more akin to that of a teacher. I am a mentor to many people, both within and outside my firm, professionally or personally. I never say no to anyone asking for mentorship. It's a very rewarding role. I meet with my mentees on a regular basis, keep abreast of what they're doing, and advise them accordingly. I guide them to resources and provide critical feedback so they can learn and grow.

When looking for a mentor, you need to understand and accept that you'll be given constructive criticism. This is an essential part of your growth. It takes strength of character to have a document you poured your soul into comes back covered in redlines. Approaching mentorship with the attitude that you're already the best at what you do and have nothing to learn is completely useless. It's misplaced cockiness, no matter your age or career stage. Yes, your ego will take a hit, but remember that your mentor took time away from their work to review yours and redline it. They did this to help you and teach you. Be grateful, hold your chin up, and go back to the drawing board with the confidence that someone has your back and wants you to be great at what you do.

When I was a young lawyer, my work got redlined all the time. And you know what? It still does, even after thirty-two years of practice. I don't take it personally. In fact, I look for it. I embrace it. It has helped me immensely. The best lawyers and litigators in the field do mock trials before launching into the real courtroom for a reason: everyone, without exception, can improve their work product. I accept the redlining, corrections, and feedback. If you do this, you'll understand the mentoring process. At the end of the day, those who refuse to accept criticism will not reach the top of their game.

A champion is different. You need to find and solicit someone who will be your champion. They won't be assigned to you. Do not assume your mentor will also be your champion—this is a completely different role. A peer can be a mentor, but a champion requires a bit more gravitas. As we advance in our careers, no matter the field, we often forget the importance of surrounding ourselves with champions. We think we've outgrown that phase of our professional lives and can succeed on our own. Wrong! The importance of surrounding yourself with champions, both in your professional and personal life, never stops. It remains crucial.

A champion is someone who actively promotes you. They provide speaking and publishing opportunities, introduce you to their network, expand your connections, sell you, help you get promotions, defend you, and promote you to others. In other words, they're your biggest fans and go to bat for you. That's a champion. That's not the same as mentorship. Mentoring is teaching. Championing is giving you opportunities and opening doors, but you must be willing to walk through them.

Most often, the best champions are also the busiest people. You need to speak up. Ask questions and be specific about what you want to accomplish, why you think they can be your champion, and why they should support you.

As a woman, I would argue that having men as your champions can be highly beneficial. Don't get me wrong, gender has nothing to do with the ability to champion someone; however, having the opposite sex in your corner can speak volumes. This holds true regardless of your gender or how you identify. Having champions from "the opposite team" is very helpful and sends a powerful message.

I have been incredibly fortunate to have many champions in my life. From the age of twenty-three, at the beginning of my career, I vividly recall a senior partner who made it a point to keep me in mind for key opportunities. He invited me to attend cocktail parties or events in the legal profession with him, and he actively worked the room for me. He didn't need to work the room for himself because he was already well known, but he would say to each key person there, "Let me introduce you to this great up-and-coming superstar." This active promotion allowed me to develop an extensive network in my early years, all thanks to having him being my champion.

Later, when I moved to Toronto in 2006, a colleague of mine at Ogilvy Renault couldn't understand how I had achieved all these legal rankings after just thirteen years of practice. It puzzled him that he had none of these rankings, despite the fact that he deserved them. He was a fantastic and accomplished colleague, and it wasn't that I was better than him. It was entirely due to having a champion throughout my career. Someone who made sure I was ranked each year, and that my work was recognized, mentioned, or talked about. Then it snowballed, like a wheel gaining momentum. My colleague didn't have that privilege, or perhaps he didn't realize he could have such a person in his life.

Now, I do this for lawyers on my team who ask me to be their champion, and even for those who don't formally ask, but whom I feel could benefit from active promotion. I ensure they get speaking or publishing opportunities. I introduce them to clients to promote them. In recent years, I gave up a lot of my leadership roles with different legal organizations to pass the responsibilities on to others who were building their profile in the profession. My focus is very much on ensuring a healthy succession and allowing the next generation to shine. As I said, it's a wheel—it must keep rolling.

When it was announced that I would be writing this book, I was overwhelmed by the number of messages I received from many young women I didn't even know. They said things like, "You're my role model in the market," and "I can't wait to read the book because I look up to you, and I feel lost right now." While it was flattering, I felt a bit of imposter syndrome again reading those personal notes, but it also made me realize how many young women still don't have enough champions in their life. They crave that support, and they need it.

Many have approached me in the past, asking how I managed my career and family, and still had time for eleven horses, three dogs and vacations to our house in Italy, or anywhere else. I'm a firm believer that I would not have accomplished any of it had it not been for the champions in my life at various stages. They served as the diving board into the pool of opportunity.

I often get requests to go for coffee and chat about one's career. However, there's a difference between coming to me and saying, "I want to be successful, help me do that," and coming prepared with an outline, specific goals, and a plan. Know what your next steps are and then seek help to achieve them. Identify your short-term, medium-term, and long-term goals, and then ask, "Is there anything you can do to help me? Can you introduce me to this person or that person?"

Asking for help requires some guts and humility. People often worry that they'll be perceived as having a big ego if they ask such things. Women, in particular, often feel like they'll seem cocky if they ask. This is not true; on the contrary.

A lawyer at my firm followed this process perfectly. He asked to go for coffee, outlined what he wanted to do, and asked, "What should I do first? Can you help me refine my plan?" He was well prepared and had clearly thought this through. I was so impressed. It can be daunting because people often think, "Why would that person make time for me?" Yes, I am busy, but I will make time for you. If you ask me to be your champion, I will make the time. It's important to me, and I'm not unique in that regard. A lot of successful people will react the same way. It may be surprising to find out how eager successful people are to help others achieve the same level of success. The notion that busy people don't have time to be champions is a myth.

Sometimes, the best champions in your life will come from unexpected places. When I arrived in Toronto in 2006, I recall meeting a partner from a competing firm at one of my very first cocktail parties. He asked how I was doing, and I said, "I'm doing okay, but I don't have my sea legs yet. I feel a bit lost because it's a strange feeling not knowing anybody in this room." That was all I needed to say. He introduced me to the Advocates' Society, saying, "If you want to know who you need to know in this market, become a member of the Advocates' Society and get involved. Become a skills instructor. You'll meet a ton of people. Collegiality is key, and the Society holds plenty of social events. You won't feel lost for long."

This transparent conversation with a lawyer from another firm helped me rebuild my network quickly. I joined the Society and eventually helped create the Quebec division of this amazing organization so Quebec lawyers could benefit from what had served me so well when I arrived in Toronto. I also became a national board member.

It all stemmed from that one conversation where I admitted to feeling lost. He told me what to do, and then I took the ball and ran with it. Make no mistake, at that moment, he was my champion—my key to developing my Toronto network.

Remember my nomination by a competitor to become a member of the International Association of Defense Counsel? The same thing applied. It was one moment in time. I asked, and he took the time to prepare my nomination and find sponsors. There was nothing in it for him. Through that gesture, he became my champion.

Other champions in my professional life have been long-standing relationships. At Ogilvy Renault, John Coleman was one of them, and so was the partner I mentioned earlier. After I joined Torys, Les Viner certainly became a champion for me, and so were most of my new partners. I am blessed to belong to a firm where everyone champions each other and is eager to help everyone else shine. Even busy partners like Sheila Block, Trisha Jackson, and Linda Plumpton were my champions at various times because they wanted me to succeed. It is a cultural thing. The list is too long to name them all, but I realize this is not the case in every organization. I refuse to believe you cannot find at least one person willing to champion you, no matter where you work or what field you're in.

Remember, champions can be one-offs. There is no one-size-fits-all mold. You can have as many champions as you need. Some will be permanent fixtures in your life, while others will come and go. However, you will not see them if you're closed-minded or don't speak up. There are no limits to what you can ask for.

When you have a champion, the most important thing is to make sure you deliver. A champion has taken time out of their busy lives, put in the effort, praised your name to others, and opened doors for you. If you don't show up and seize these opportunities, that person won't be your champion for long. They'll think you're not interested or that you're not willing to help yourself. For me, there's nothing worse than giving up my time for someone who can't be bothered to follow through. It's not just that I get frustrated over wasting my time, it's almost a sense of sadness. I opened this door for someone, but they didn't walk through it.

There's also a sense of momentum behind some things. Timing is important. If I told you to contact Mr. So-and-so because he was going to give you a position on a board, but then I find out two months later that you never made the call, it's a problem.

When a champion opens a door, you need to walk through it, or at the very least, communicate why you didn't or why you couldn't follow through. Otherwise, you risk losing your champions.

I often share this insight with my daughter. She had an opportunity to take on a leadership role at university and had committed to doing it. After some thought, she decided she had bitten off more than she could chew, and I agreed. In addition to her studies, she had several extracurricular activities and a part-time job. I told her, "You need to write back to make sure it doesn't create an inconvenience for them if you step down. They may have a waiting list of people willing to take the role. Be honest and tell them that this opportunity is going to take a bigger chunk of your time than you anticipated, but don't want to abandon them. If they have somebody else, you will let it go, but if they don't, you will stick to your commitment."

I had to tell her that. Her reaction was simply, "I have too much on my plate and need to drop this one. I'm just going to quit." You do not outright quit an opportunity, but you can justify passing on it. That way, the door remains open for you in the future. Sure enough, when Florence sent that email, the university's response was, "Thank you so much. Yes, we have a waiting list. We'll keep you in mind for the next opportunity." There is a way to decline an opportunity, but not responding is not one of them.

Don't burn bridges. Keep your connections open because life happens, and you may not realize that you weren't as ready as you thought you were to take the next step. It's all fair, but you have to be respectful of those who are opening doors for you.

This principle applies to every aspect of your life. Remember my figure skating career when my parents had no money? Clearly, there was someone championing me behind the scenes, providing financial support, and I didn't even know it. I took it for granted, but it was there.

When I was a little older, I was the captain of the synchronized skating team. I broke my ankle a couple of days before provincials, and the parents of a teammate paid for my physiotherapy because my family didn't have any insurance and certainly couldn't afford it. So, even as a child, my accomplishments, despite poverty and everything else, required a champion—someone who believed in me and wanted me to succeed.

You definitely need champions in your personal life. The biggest and most constant champion in my life has been my husband, Paul. I needed a champion at home in order to thrive at work. You require a champion in your personal life who genuinely wants you to succeed—someone who is willing to assume that secondary role, outside of the spotlight. It takes a very humble and generous person to take on that role. Paul has sometimes been called Mr. Rodrigue instead of Mr. Carenza. It doesn't bother him. He has his own share of successes and accomplishments, including a thriving legal practice. He is very secure and has often been the one holding the fort at home while I'm traveling for work. I owe a lot of my accomplishments to Paul.

Every successful person needs a strong partner who doesn't feel threatened by their success—a partner who puts them first and champions them. I have that in Paul. He is the ultimate champion in my life.

Do not underestimate the other champions in your family and close circle of friends. You likely have these individuals without even realizing it. They may be hidden or understated, but they create that feeling of knowing someone always has your back, no matter what. That's the knowledge that there is a champion for you within that circle. My baby sister, Sophie, has been my rock and my champion in family matters. She is there for me day in and day out, no matter what. My close friends Lorraine and Kieron, along with their daughters, Rachel and Catherine, are family to me.

They have been my biggest supporters and were there for me at my highest and my lowest points. As was my daughter, of course. Even though young adults don't always know how to express it, I know she champions me in various ways.

Having champions in your personal life can take different forms. For example, as Paul and I plan our long-term retirement project in Italy, he and I have gained new champions in our lives. Our friends, Alessandro and Monica, as well as our lawyer and friend, Federica, have been instrumental in helping us build a network of relationships in Italy—friends and business acquaintances—to help us feel at home and ensure were learn and respect Italian customs and practices. They've been very systemic and deliberate about this, saying, "Sylvie and Paul will love that person . . . or will need that person at some point, so I'm going to introduce that person to them during a dinner." This is what it means to be a champion for your friends. I do the same in Canada. I will not host a dinner party without a seating arrangement. It takes me hours to move the cards and figure out who should sit beside whom. I'm always thinking of who will benefit from a new connection.

A colleague who knows about our new life in Italy wondered how it would be possible for someone in their fifties to rebuild a network of friends in a foreign country. It's very difficult to rebuild a network of friends later in life, as most of your friends are anchored. I explained that the growth of our Italian network developed because one or two friends who deeply care about us deliberately made the introductions. Our network grew exactly as it did in Canada, which was the same way it grew when I was in my twenties in Montreal, and again in my forties in Toronto. All you need is a champion who starts the cycle of introductions. There's a little bit of luck involved, but I think you attract luck through your behavior—by being open, grateful, and alert to opportunities. You create your own luck to a certain extent. It's in the energy you convey. The universe works this way.

People who are champions have most likely had good champions themselves. Be bold. Seek out those who can help you. Ask for exactly what you need and show them that you have a plan. And when they provide you with the opportunity, take it. Deliver. Keep this practice in every aspect of your life where you need help to reach your goals. You will succeed, and one day, you will undoubtedly become someone else's champion. It's a role I cherish every single day.

PRACTICAL TAKEAWAYS

With respect to the goals you wrote down in the first exercise, identify the "white noise" you heard. Classify them into:

a. pessimism/negativity

_____

_____

b. jealousy

_____

_____

c. genuine concerns

_____

_____

Name at least two champions you have or would like to have, as well as two mentors. Ask them if they would like to take on that role.

_____

_____

List the names of individuals in your life whom you believe are hindering your success.

_____

_____

Make a list of goals you want your champions to help you achieve. Identify which short-, medium-, or long-term goals they can help you achieve.

_____

_____

6

LIFE IS A MARATHON, NOT A RACE

Life is truly a marathon, not a race. If you're going to build a successful career, it must be done at the right pace. Some things cannot be rushed. It's a fallacy to think that you can achieve instant success. Other than a few rare exceptions, every single success story has a long history of hard work, failing and trying again, changing directions, putting in years of effort, and having the discipline to see things through. No matter what field you're in, there is no shortcut to success.

I can understand the desire for immediate success, and there's nothing wrong with ambition. I was, and still am, very ambitious; however, I'm also quite impatient. Patience is not a virtue of mine, so I still need to work at it. Daily. But let's not confuse ambition with entitlement. You may have earned your degree, or you may have been a top performer during the first year at your new job, but that doesn't mean you'll receive instant rewards. Life doesn't work that way. Those who are truly successful earned it through years and years of hard work. In other words, you need to pay your dues.

This is true in every profession or field, though my experience is in the legal world. While I see many hard-working young professionals, it's unfortunate that I also encounter a sense of entitlement in some. I do not want to generalize—not every young lawyer has a sense of entitlement—but I've seen some individuals who feel that if they aren't offered an appointment to the partnership within their self-imposed time frame, they go across the street to another firm that will give them the coveted title. This is short-sighted and unfortunate.

I firmly believe in building your career over time, with the proper building blocks: experience, skill development, and earning trust. Believe and trust that you will become highly regarded; opportunities will come your way. There will be no need to demand them, because your work will eventually speak for itself—and it will speak loudly. There will be no doubt about your capabilities, potential, or worth. It will just be known. In the end, work ethic conquers all obstacles and is the only true way to achieve your goals.

While waiting for opportunities may appear to contradict the lesson about being the master of your own destiny, it does not. These are two different concepts. You can be the conductor of your life while understanding that not everything will be handed to you in your first year on the job.

The truth is, life doesn't owe you anything. We live in a culture of instantaneity, where everything happens now and happens fast. Contrast that sense of entitlement with when I wanted that law student summer position back in 1989. I absolutely deserved to get that position, and I absolutely deserved to be offered a position as a lawyer, and to eventually become a partner. However, it never crossed my mind that I was entitled. I was nervous and had doubts each time. Maybe I should have had more faith in the fact that I had earned what I was being offered. Maybe I should have been more assertive and had fewer doubts. That's on me, but you need to find the right balance between putting in the work, earning your successes, and what legitimately entitles you to a promotion or a specific position.

The reality is that you need perspective. You may do everything you can to earn that promotion and still not get it, but that shouldn't be the end of the world. It should not send you spiraling into negativity or lower self-esteem to the point that you believe you're not in the right job. On the contrary, that is real life. It's a bump on the road. You fall, and you get back up again. That is the right cycle.

Talk to any successful person and they'll tell you they've all experienced defeat and setbacks. Having a sense of entitlement early in your career prevents growth. It hinders your ability to use defeats as learning opportunities and makes you weak, not strong. Each stage of your career and personal life has its purpose, containing invaluable lessons that test and challenge you. They push you to see if you can make the right choices at the right time so you can have the life and career you really want. You can't rush through this, and you shouldn't want to. The image of immediate success is a fallacy. There is no such thing.

I understand the desire for immediate respect. I wanted to argue at the Supreme Court of Canada right away when I started my career so I'd earn the judges' respect and have the gravitas and credibility of my senior colleagues. However, jumping too quickly can jeopardize your career, not advance it. Baby steps may seem more cautious, but they build a much more stable road than any leaps could achieve.

Embrace the learning curve, don't despise it. Again, your career is a marathon, not a race. I say this often to all the young lawyers on my team who wonder how they should approach business development at their level. They don't know where to start building their network. They feel somehow handicapped because they don't have the pull or gravitas to invite decision-makers for lunch or dinner. This is because they look too far ahead, skipping important steps and wanting to emulate what their senior colleagues are doing.

You don't have to invite the CEO or General Counsel of a client for dinner in your first year of practice—perhaps not even in your fifth year. Rather, pay attention to the junior lawyer in their mid-to late-twenties from the client's in-house legal department. That junior will grow alongside you, progressing in parallel with your own career. One day, they may be the one hiring you to lead a file.

Relationships are key to your career, and they are built overtime. You can't achieve everything in your first years on the job. Some people achieve success faster than others, but they still need to earn it. Go at your own rhythm and it will all fall into place in due course. But you need to be deliberate about it.

Make your success plan. Figure out what you need to reach the next level and eventually get where you want to be. Break down your goals into short-term, medium-term, and long-term objectives. You cannot go immediately from earning your degree to achieving your long-term goal.

After graduating, I wrote down each of my goals and put them on a wall in my study at home to serve as reminders. My short-term goal was to acquire as many skills as I could. I wanted to become a great litigator, so I surrounded myself with great mentors and teachers to learn from. This included perfecting my English. At age twenty-three, I could speak well enough, but I struggled with writing. I certainly couldn't crossexamine an English-speaking witness. This was a significant obstacle for me.

I also focused on the art of preparation and aimed to excel at the tasks assigned to me, no matter how small they were. It didn't matter whether it was a short memo, letter, or phone call, I made sure it was as perfect as possible, given my level of experience.

I still remember my very first appearance in court. I had to argue a small, uncontested motion, but I completely over prepared for it. Just like at my figure skating program at the Quebec games, I was determined to deliver it perfectly. I quickly learned that, as a litigator, preparation is everything. It always makes me laugh when people say to me, "You're such a great public speaker," or "You're so eloquent in court." They assume it just comes naturally. If only they knew how much time I practice in front of the mirror.

To this day, I still practice important presentations in front of the mirror. Always. You sound it out, adjust, edit, and start again. The same goes with speeches. Some people can improvise, but it's rare. Most skilled public speakers rehearse extensively before performing because, make no mistake, it is a performance.

I also set specific goals from a business development perspective to grow my profile and establish a name for myself. For example, as our South American client base grew, I took Spanish courses so I could communicate with clients in their mother tongue, thinking it would give me an edge. Looking ahead, I was trying to set myself apart. I also noticed that lawyers were playing golf with clients, albeit mostly male lawyers, so I learned to play golf. Given the increasing number of women in leadership positions among our clientele, I thought it would be beneficial to plan some women-only initiatives. This may seem obvious now, but it was not in 1993. If you take the time to identify a void in your current field, you will find something to fill it. That's why writing down your goals and planning how to reach them is so important. Success will not fall from the sky. Nothing does.

I attended as many networking events as possible, published articles, and lobbied to be invited as a speaker at various conferences. I did nothing on my own. Instead, I approached the people I believed could help me achieve these short-terms goals, which set me up for success long-term. I gain skills, recognition, and respect, and I developed an outstanding reputation amongst my peers, opposing counsel, and the Bench. You can't start building your profile and reputation ten years into your career; it starts on day one.

I made mistakes along the way—small ones, and big ones—but each was a learning opportunity. One major error stemmed from my ambition to climb the ladder too fast. My inexperience and cockiness blinded me, leading me to believe gender equality meant I could do things the same way my male colleagues did. I come from the first generation of law school classes where there were more female students than male. By age twenty-four, I was fortunate to have not faced gender discrimination, so it never crossed my mind that I should act any differently than my male colleagues or senior female partners. To me, seniority and gender were completely irrelevant in how I should conduct myself as a professional—or so I thought.

Early in my career, I noticed that my male colleagues regularly took clients out for dinner or to hockey games, which seemed like a great way to develop relationships. Why shouldn't I do the same?

We had a client from the United States, an older gentleman in his sixties, and I was the junior lawyer to a female partner who'd taken his file. I did as my male colleagues did and invited the client for dinner, one-on-one, to show my appreciation and thank him for his loyalty to the firm. It backfired. Big time.

He interpreted the invitation to dinner as a date. His hands were under the table, grabbing my legs, and he wanted to go dancing or for a drink on Crescent Street, a party street in Montreal. I tried to get away from him and find a way out, but because he was a significant client for the firm, so I couldn't just be rude and leave him. I felt conflicted between my obligation as a professional and my instinct as a twenty-four-year-old woman to just slap this guy in the face.

This happened long before the Me Too movement. Back in 1994, there were still plenty of men who weren't concerned about being reported for inappropriate behavior. I didn't follow my instinct as a woman. I thought, "My colleagues do this, so I need to do this," and I prioritized the firm's reputation. We ended up on Crescent Street, and I thought, "Okay, I'll have one drink, and then leave." But then, he wanted to slow dance. At that point, I bolted and ran back to the office with him chasing me down the street. It was like a scene out of a parody.

It's the funniest anecdote, completely ridiculous, really. I share this story for two reasons. First, the morning after the incident, I swallowed my pride and found the courage to go see the partner responsible for that client and tell her what had happened. Being female, she completely supported me. She called the client the next day and gave him a piece of her mind. I don't know if we ever worked for this client again, but she defended me. She had my back. That female partner was already a champion for me in my career. It didn't matter that this was a big client; she didn't question it. She took my side.

Second, the lesson is that I was trying, at twenty-four, to act like a senior lawyer with gravitas and experience. I thought I knew it all and that I was invincible, but I was too arrogant and moved too fast.

The bottom line is that if you leap too far forward without doing the legwork and without the proper experience, you will experience failure. I was lucky I had a champion who helped me, but it could have easily gone the other way. It could have ruined my career. You don't want to self-destruct before you've even begun.

After that episode, I realized I didn't have to act like a man to be successful. I could do business development my way—the female way—and not the way a fifty-year-old would do it either. I changed my ways. Unless I knew the client really well, which I didn't at that young age, I invited other colleagues or spouses to join me for dinner with the client. I set my eagerness aside and adjusted how I did things.

I upheld this approach until I grew into my role. I adopted the marathon pace. Women may feel this is unfair, wondering why they feel the need to act differently. It's not derogatory, and it's not about feeling less capable than a man or a senior partner. You can be just as successful while doing things differently—doing things your way, at your level of seniority.

My medium-term goal was to be promoted to partner and to continue handling bigger and more important cases as the lead lawyer. You cannot become a partner in a law firm without having a solid business plan for generating longterm business. To achieve this, you need recognition. You need to become the go-to person for clients in your field. That's the natural progression from your short-term goals, but it all starts from having done the work from day one. No one wakes up after six years on the job and says they want to become a partner the following year. It requires planning. While my experiences have been solely in the legal world, I am confident that planning and putting in the work before reaching certain career milestones is a staple in any field of work.

While I wanted to be a partner, what I wanted most was to be respected and recognized as a great litigator. As the professional awards and recognitions started coming in after seven to eight years of practice, I started to see the fruits of my labor—much more than just receiving a title. The rankings by my peers and clients as a recognized top litigator confirmed that I had achieved my medium-term goals.

My long-term professional goals were a continuation of the medium-term goals. I wanted a sustainable, rewarding career filled with stimulating and interesting work, surrounded by great colleagues, while maintaining respect from both the Bench and the Bar. Most of all, I wanted to be happy. I sought a work-life balance and aimed to have it all—a fantastic and fulfilling career, a family with children, and a happy, well-rounded life. I did that. I have that. However, you cannot attain all of this within year one of graduating. It takes years of hard work to get there.

Be careful not to confuse ambition with entitlement. I have always been very ambitious, knowing I had the talent to succeed. I wasn't afraid to ask for help or rise to challenges. I argued my first Court of Appeal case when I was still an articling student. The partner believed I could do it, and I did. When I wanted to create the class action practice group and approached the senior partner who led the department to say we needed such a group, that wasn't entitlement, nor was it wanting to rush my career advancement. I didn't say to this partner, "I want a team, and you need to appoint me because I deserve it." Rather, I just presented my idea. They agreed it was a good idea and gave me the lead.

Some people climb the corporate ladder faster than others, and that's okay. However, very few will reach the pinnacle of their career and achieve all their goals after just one year on the job. Have patience—or, as my Italian friends would say, *piano piano*, which is a common and quintessentially Italian phrase that means slowly, slowly.

You can have drive and ambition. I had both in spades. Be ambitious and voice what you want, but do it without a sense of entitlement. I have young colleagues who do this very well. One lawyer on my team approached me the moment he joined our firm and asked to go for coffee. He identified his short-, medium-, and long-term goals and asked what I thought he should do and what he should focus on. This was the perfect way to do it. He didn't come across as entitled and didn't insist we make him partner. Eventually, he made partner, but he earned it through hard work. There's a nuanced difference between seeking help to build your foundation and feeling entitled to your ultimate goal without putting the building blocks in place to earn it.

It doesn't matter what your profession is. If I look back at everything I've accomplished—from earning top grades to get into law school, from the grind in law school to getting hired at the best firm, and from putting in the work to become a partner—it all came down to discipline. I had to work long hours to achieve each milestone. Rebuilding my career in Toronto after thirteen years as a Quebec lawyer and opening Torys Montreal office didn't happen overnight, and certainly not without hard work. I don't know any successful people, male or female, who didn't work hard to achieve their professional goals. Instant millionaires are a myth. Yes, the right idea, the right time, and the right market speeds up success, but most successful people work hard all day, every day.

This may appear to contradict some points I made in previous chapters, but it doesn't. You can be fearless, not let imposter syndrome paralyze you, and be the master of your own destiny while maintaining a strong work ethic and understanding the need to earn success one step at a time. Sometimes your decisions will produce immediate results. Sometimes your ideas will propel you to the next level. However, none of it will happen without putting in the work. That is the point.

This principle also applies to your personal life. Success doesn't fall from the sky. It requires time, effort, and discipline, no matter what your personal goals are. I've had a lot of setbacks and failures in life. They're a part of life. You cannot expect only success, and especially not quick success. You will fail, but you will also learn.

When it comes to matters of the heart, that's when it can be difficult to remain disciplined. As mentioned earlier, I had three long-term relationships before meeting Paul, and I left all of them because they were hindering my pursuit of happiness. Emotional difficulties aside, it was easier to leave the first two relationships because we didn't have a mortgage or children. When I met Florence's father, I was just renting an apartment and still didn't have much to my name. Diego was a good person. He was family oriented, and I liked his family. There was a sense of security with him. I knew we could have a family together. That same year, I became a partner at my firm and we moved in together. We eventually got married and bought a house.

I know firsthand how deeply personal setbacks can impact one's life. Being adopted, it was extremely important for me to have my own child and to experience that bond between mother and child. After those three miscarriages, I could have given up or played the victim, believing it would never happen. I'm not Superwoman, so I can be vulnerable. I can fall. And I did. My mind clung to the belief that my biological mother had abandoned me—that she didn't want me. She didn't want a child, and I wanted one, but couldn't have one. Why me? It all felt so unfair. At some point, I accepted reality.

I felt destroyed, yet I found the strength to stand up again. I truly believe everyone has this ability. It's unclear to me what it is that forces some people to get back on their feet, but not others. Part of it is a positive attitude, but you must also allow yourself to feel what you're feeling when you get knocked down. Embrace those "poor me" and "why me?" feelings. Don't deny yourself the time to go through that. Allow yourself to cry, to feel depressed. It's not human to suppress those emotions, but don't linger in that state there long.

I wanted to throw in the towel many times, but I snapped out of it. That's the difference between those who get back up and those who don't. Snap out of it. Plan your next step and stay focused. Do you know what your next step is? Once you regain hope, try again. I was determined to have this child. So, I tried again.

The doctor I mentioned earlier, Dr. Alice Benjamin, sent the last fetus for an autopsy to determine the cause of death. It turned out that all my babies had suffered strokes. I realized I should never have been on the pill as a young woman, as I could have had a stroke myself. Thankfully, I didn't, but my babies weren't so fortunate.

When I became pregnant again, Dr. Benjamin put me on baby aspirin and monitored me closely. She assured me we could do this, reigniting my motivation to achieve my dream of having a child.

The hospital was just up the hill from my office. I went up that hill every two weeks for checkups and followed all the doctor's precautions. I diligently drank those five glasses of milk per day, took naps, and avoided alcohol and coffee. I was on a mission. This time, it was going to work.

In total, it took four years to bring one baby into the world. It was truly a marathon. My gorgeous Florence was born on January 19, 2004. She put me through thirty-one hours of labor only to arrive by cesarean section, as she'd been in distress. Nonetheless, she was worth every minute and all the work and discipline I put into that pregnancy. I never gave up, and I was richly rewarded with the biggest and most important reward of them all.

My marathon continued with Florence's father, but we eventually decided to split to pursue our respective professional goals. When I met Paul, that relationship also required discipline and hard work so we could be happy together and create a thriving blended family. I did the work and made sacrifices every day, and I have zero regrets.

I had a dream, and I chased after it. Creating a family with four kids under the age of twelve while navigating a career across two provinces was no small feat, but it worked. My happiness has been a labor of love from day one. No one handed it to me. I pursued it, and I continue to do so.

Working and building at a snail's pace is not failure. It's carefully establishing the solid foundation for your life. Whether professionally or personally, know what your goals are and how to achieve them. Plan, plan, plan. If you fail, try again. But remember, it's on you. Step by step—it's not a race. It's a marathon.

7

YOU CAN HAVE IT ALL

Women who enter the workforce while simultaneously carrying the responsibility of having a family are often told, "You can't have it all." It implies that something's got to give, because you can't be 100 percent devoted to both your professional and personal life. Society has made us believe we cannot be successful in both aspects simultaneously, but I completely disagree. The idea that you must sacrifice your career to have a happy family life, or vice versa, is a myth.

Throughout my career, many people have assumed that because I'm successful professionally, I must not have much of a family life, or a family at all. For twenty-one years, I have been a very present, very involved mother. My daughter was a competitive Irish dancer, an eventing rider, and a boxer. From the time she was five until she turned eighteen, I travelled extensively with her for competitions across all three sports. I made the time and made it work.

I now have elderly parents who need care, which demands time. Plus, over the years, I've had to care for eleven horses and a few dogs, and I keep an active social life. In the last ten years, Paul and I have enjoyed a second social life in Tuscany, where we have a farmhouse. We have a very busy, but very happy life. It works.

Thus, I do not subscribe to the belief that you can only have either a career or a family to be truly happy and successful. It can be difficult to succeed in every aspect of life, and it does take a lot of hard work and organization. I will not sugarcoat this reality. It is possible. Achieving balance requires directing traffic, asking for help, choosing the right partner, selecting the right workplace, and accepting that there will always be some guilt involved. You must establish boundaries and keep them, and you must recognize that you cannot accomplish this alone. Alone, you cannot have it all, but with the right support in your life, you can. It's like a giant puzzle: each part has its importance. It's intricate and tricky, but when all the pieces are in the right places, it can paint a picture of a beautiful life.

It's crucial to surround yourself with the right people, both in your personal and professional life. There is no way I'd have been able to go through all the setbacks if I didn't have the right support network around me. Some of the essential support I received came from the people I worked with. By the age of thirty-two, I was already a partner, and for the next two years, I was basically pregnant all the time. During my pregnancy with Florence, I still had to perform at work, despite being at the doctor's office every two weeks to check on the baby's heartbeat. Yet, I maintained a successful career while nurturing a high-risk pregnancy. How? Support. The female partner who'd helped me out with the handsy client came with me to the hospital for my ultrasound because I was always afraid of finding out there was no heartbeat. Emotional support at home and work was key to getting through that difficult period.

I remember having a couch delivered to my office so I could take naps. My colleagues knew not to bother me between 1 and 3:00 p.m. I wasn't afraid to share what was happening in my life during my pregnancy. The work was getting done, but on my time. I did some work at 5:00 a.m.

because I'm an early bird, but after lunch I'd be napping, and at 4:00 p.m., I was at the hospital for checkups. I kept up with my hard work and met all my deadlines. For my pregnancy to be a success, I had to take charge of how that would happen. Despite daily work stress, I stayed on top of things and completed all my tasks.

I can hear some skeptics saying, "But you were a partner, an associate couldn't do that." That is simply not true. It's within your power to surround yourself with the right people. Go find that champion we talked about—someone to advocate for you. Make a plan and then propose that plan. I promise you can have it all. This has nothing to do with hierarchy.

When I moved to Toronto and had four children to care for on some days, I was also directing a lot of traffic, but I wasn't doing it alone. I didn't have to direct Paul. He was my true partner. I didn't have to ask because he intuitively knew what had to be done. I think that's why we've been together now for twenty years. It's crucial to have the right partner in your life if you want to have it all. Paul takes initiative. If I complain that my phone keeps freezing, there's a new phone waiting for me on the kitchen counter the next day. I never have to ask.

He is extraordinary. That's what true life partnership looks like.

I have experienced two important periods in my adult life when time management became crucial: the time before Paul when I was a single mother, and the time after when I had a larger nuclear family. When I was alone, my adoptive mother helped out with Florence. I had to work all day, but from 5:00 p.m. to 8:00 p.m., I was offline because I wanted to be with my daughter and put her to bed. Once she was asleep, if there was work to do, I'd be back online. I established boundaries and chose how to organize myself in order to have it all.

Yes, I felt guilty at times. People may judge you for being offline for a few hours, and you might think, "I can't possibly do that without letting my career suffer." So, you feel obliged to stay at work late. But then you feel guilty because your nanny is upset about having to stay late, and your children are upset they didn't see you before bed. You feel you are disappointing everyone.

There will always be guilt. I always felt it, and I accepted that it would be part of my reality. There are ways to overcome guilt. You cannot let the feeling prevent you from organizing your life or focusing on quality over quantity.

After moving in with Paul, we hired a nanny—never a live-in one, as I needed my personal space. We had the most amazing woman who I called "Mary Poppins" because she was from the UK. Her name was Julie, just like Julie Andrews, and she stayed with us for thirteen years. We felt it was important to have someone who spoke English and could "be me" when I was at work. It takes a lot of humility to set aside your ego and allow someone to be you when you're not there. It's hard, but I didn't want someone to just *watch* Florence; I wanted someone who could attend the library coffee at school, help with homework, volunteer for school trips, and do the things I couldn't do. I wanted a duplicate of myself at home for my daughter, and that was tough.

Some women will feel insecure and fear that the nanny will replace them. There's an element of emotional sacrifice involved. I still showed up for every concert, school play, presentation, and parent-teacher interview. Those things just had to be my things. I prioritized and made my choices accordingly.

Not only did I have Paul at home at night when I was traveling for work, but I had the right support in Julie. And yes, there were times when I would show up with Julie at my daughter's school when she was in kindergarten or Grade one, and other mothers would be confused, realizing Julie wasn't Florence's mother. Those moments hurt, I chose my daughter's happiness over my insecurities and need for control.

This arrangement worked perfectly because Julie was there for every parent-required event and, when I could, we attended together. However, Julie was still the one driving Florence to school every day, taking her to dance classes, cooking meals, and doing laundry. She was the one doing the things I couldn't do.

I like to think that I was lucky to find someone as extraordinary as Julie, who eventually became a part of our family. I don't think our situation was unique. While not everyone can afford a nanny—and I can certainly relate to that, given my upbringing—there are other ways to achieve similar support.

Friends and family members can be a big help. It might also involve organizing your life around public service schedules, as long as you keep the lines of communication open with your employer concerning your schedule. The key point is: no one can do it all alone. You need support, and that support takes various forms.

If you contrast the choices I made regarding my need to have a biological child because of my adoption, it may seem a bit off to accept that I'd be okay with someone else taking my place when I wasn't home. However, that was my way of having it all. With Julie's support, my daughter was happy, and I had no trust issues, which allowed me to focus on my career while knowing I had someone at home I could trust.

I still had a crazy schedule, flying back and forth between Montreal and Toronto, sometimes on the same day, just so I could put Florence to bed myself. That aligns with the idea of quality time versus quantity. When I couldn't have that quality time with her, my guilt was alleviated because I had found the right person to care for her.

Many young lawyers ask me, "How the hell did you do it?" especially when my daughter began competitive dancing. Soon after she started Irish dancing, Florence was on the podium at competitions, and she wasn't even eight years old yet. As with any dance, the training was intense, from fifteen to twenty hours a week, with competitions multiple times a month—locally, nationally, and internationally.

She then began training in the UK. From 2008 to 2017, I was with Florence at every single competition, except one. We were on the road almost every weekend. I remember being in roadside motels with her a lot, and doing her hair and makeup. While she was training, I would be at the motel working. It was never a vacation, but I didn't skip a beat.

We made it work. It puzzled a lot of young lawyers how it was even possible to be a partner with all these family responsibilities while traveling almost every weekend to be with my daughter. I made deliberate choices and wouldn't schedule a court hearing the Friday before a weekend competition. I adjusted my work schedule to make sure I could be with her. Our quality time happened the day of her competition. I would set an out-of-office message so my colleagues would know not to disturb me. My daughter understood that I still had to work on our road trips, but when she was on stage, I was 100 percent there for her.

Despite my demanding career, I create quality time with my daughter when she was growing up. Those nights in motels before competitions were bonding experiences. It was often just her and me, because Paul was at home with the boys and our dogs. He held the fort when I was away with Florence. That's how my daughter and I became so close. Although Florence may have only seen me for an hour or so before bedtime during the week, our trips for dance, horse shows, and boxing competitions created fond memories.

I mentioned missing only one competition, and that was a conscious decision. It coincided with my first retreat with Torys. I had just joined the firm, and it was an excellent opportunity to meet everyone from the other offices. The retreat was in Phoenix, Arizona, and Florence was competing at the Great Britain Championship that weekend.

The time difference between Phoenix and the UK was eight hours. It was extremely hard to let her go and relinquish being in charge, considering she was only eleven years old. Julie went with her, but I had to manage my control-freak tendencies, trust another parent to do Florence's hair and makeup, and trust Julie to put her to bed at a decent time.

I had to trust the team around Florence. They were all great, of course. Ironically, she ended up earning her best international results that weekend. People said it was because I wasn't there. Maybe she felt less pressure, although I felt the pressure immensely.

A friend of mine, the mother of another dancer, texted me live updates throughout the event, whether Florence was backstage, on stage, or seeing the results. It was nerve-wracking, but I had to trust those around her to keep me informed while I focused on my work event. That weekend, I prioritized work and gave control to others. It was a difficult move, but I did it. My daughter? She was probably happier without her stressed-out mom there. Win-win!

If you want to do it all but don't have help or don't want to ask for help, you'll never have it all. If you never say no to anyone and try to meet everyone's expectations, then you will ultimately fail. Instead, set realistic expectations for yourself, your team, and your support systems. I kept organized every day, and I worked hard to make it all work. It's not easy, but it is possible.

Another important area of life that requires balance is your relationship. Paul and I are a team, and we need to care for each other and our relationship. We didn't have weekly date nights like many couples. Our busy careers, commitments to the kids, and last-minute work schedule changes made that impractical. However, we took about three vacations a year. Just us. No kids. Our time away was a real escape because Julie's help at home with the kids allowed us some much-needed quality time together. While we may not have had a higher quantity of date nights throughout the year, we always booked our trips in advance, so we had a full week of alone-time every three to four months to look forward to.

We both share a love for music, rooted in my skating days and Paul's time as a DJ before he became a lawyer. His parents were also professional ballroom dancers, so music and dancing have always been our escape. We entertained a lot on Friday and Saturday nights, and even after our guests left, we would dance alone in the kitchen, enjoying our quality time together. This is our bond, and the lyrics to songs mean a lot to us. It's how we talk to each other sometimes. It's our romance.

Despite our busy lives, Paul and I still went to the kids' activities, took care of our dogs, horses, and our beautiful country home. We did and continue to do so many things together. We make the time. We are a team.

Planning was essential. I won't sugarcoat it—it required a lot of work. Every busy household juggles activities like dance competitions, soccer games, concerts, and horse shows. The ability to have it all isn't a walk in the park. It requires sacrifice and acceptance of guilt, which will always be there, but you can manage it.

One thing is certain: I wouldn't have managed the last twenty years if I didn't have the right partner. When I broke down in 2024, it was because I was taking on too much. With no boundaries in place, I slowly slipped into becoming a yes-woman.

I never put myself first, and that eventually brought me down. When you try to meet everyone's expectations, you lose control of your own life. Ironically, it's because you're trying to maintain control by holding on to every responsibility that you end up running yourself into the ground, believing you can be everywhere at once and do everything for everyone.

Thus, the ability to have it all involves learning to set boundaries. Know when to say yes and when to say no. Stay organized and eliminate unnecessary responsibilities. Lean on others, let them know what you need from them, and accept that guilt will be part of the process. It's better to have quality time you than to scramble for quantity and not even enjoy it.

Lastly, maintain your standards. I have Paul in my life because I wouldn't accept less than my standards. It was hard to leave my prior relationships because there were no major problems, such as abuse or neglect, but I knew that staying with them wouldn't give me the life I wanted. I had standards for my family, work, and personal life, and I lived up to them because I knew what would make me happy. Despite having to catch flights every week, I was determined to tuck my child into bed. I was going to spend weekends with Paul. Tired or not, I got up and went back to the airport.

It's important to note that you don't need to be in a relationship to succeed or have it all. This is in the context of wanting a career *and* a family. You must define what "having it all" means to you. For some people, it means traveling; for others, it could mean devoting their time to a charitable cause, a sport, or an art. Once you understand your goals, you take the necessary steps to make them happen. The advice about building a support network applies across all these contexts.

Life has its ups and downs for everyone. You get through them with hard work, but also because you established the proper support system around you. Only then can you truly have it all and own it!

8

KINDNESS IS YOUR ALLY: ALWAYS PAY IT FORWARD

Gratitude. Many books have been written about it, or about kindness, or how to nourish your soul and live a happy life. You might wonder what this has to do with taking ownership of your life. The connection is profound. Kindness has been at the center of my personal and professional life. I have greatly benefited from the kindness of others throughout my life, and I am grateful to so many—those who helped me directly, or in the background. Those who championed me, mentored me, and continue to do so. I owe so much to Paul, my daughter, my stepsons, my family, friends, and colleagues. I could write an entire book about the importance of gratitude; however, I want to focus on the role of kindness in your quest for success and happiness, and the importance of paying it forward, which are key aspects of my life.

We obviously know we should be kind to one another, yet in the business or professional world, there's a perpetual myth that you must be ruthless and selfish to be successful. With no regard for hurting others along the way, you must keep your eyes on the "success ball," even if it means damaging relationships.

Some of the most successful people in the world are rumored to have been difficult people to deal with—bullies who built a culture of fear around them. They showed no qualms about stepping on others to get to the top. I believe this is not only a myth but also a harmful misconception for anyone striving for a balanced and happy life. You can absolutely rise to the top of your field without it coming at the cost of another's success.

It's a difficult lesson to learn. Sometimes you have to let go of an opportunity if, in the long run, it's going to jeopardize someone else's future. Let's not confuse ambition with the need to climb over people. Ambition is your drive; it's knowing where you're going and staying in control of your destiny. However, having ambition does not mean stepping on toes to reach your final destination. It's about respect—for yourself and others. Every person can be a potential partner or an ally in the future. This applies not only in your career, but in your personal life.

I believe in humanity, and I believe most people don't wake up in the morning with a plan to be mean or disrespectful. Those who do are likely miserable, unhappy people. The more they crush others, the more they reflect their own unhappiness. Deep down, they may not know they're unhappy, but there's often a darkness hidden in deeply insecure people. In fact, the more insecure people are, the more they want to crush other people, because that's what makes them feel better about themselves. However, that is not the key to a happy, successful, fulfilling life, and it's not good for the soul. Most human beings are happier when they're kind to others, and we instill this principle in children early on.

A few years ago, I accepted the role of chair of the Salvation Army fundraising campaign for a women's and children's shelter in Montreal. This was my way of paying it forward, having benefited from the Salvation Army's generosity as a child with food and clothing. Each year, when my daughter was still very young, I took her to the shelter to bring gifts for the women and children. We would shop together for specific gifts based on a list of residents, considering their ages, genders, and needs. At just five or six years old, after giving those gifts to the women and children, Florence would say, "It feels so good to give, and I feel so much better giving people gifts than when I get gifts." Even as a child, she understood that kindness is good for the soul.

As you take control of your own destiny and reach your goals, it's important to keep kindness in mind throughout the entire process. Sometimes not taking an opportunity because it's better to let someone else have it will pay off in the long run. The person you choose to pass the opportunity to may become an ally. They will remember even twenty years later that you give them their opportunity and may become a client or a valuable personal or professional connection. That person may also eventually do the same thing for someone else. Benefiting from kindness often leads to paying that kindness forward, and that's what it's all about.

No matter what world your business is in, this principle applies. I don't have a single example to share where it didn't pay off to promote someone else. Take advantage of opportunities, but let go of an opportunity once in a while. Your success should never come at the expense of someone else. I can't think of a single instance when promoting someone else had negative consequences.

People often say to me, "You must not sleep well, you have so many balls in the air." But when my head hits the pillow, I fall asleep because I'm at peace. There's something very peaceful about doing things that are good for the soul, being well-rounded and kind to people, and championing others.

Second, do not underestimate the power of paying it forward. I addressed in a previous chapter the importance of finding yourself a champion and a mentor. Now, I'm often on the other side of that coin where I am the mentor and champion to others. I'm happy to be generous in this role because I was once the beneficiary of it. That's the pay-it-forward part—a wheel that keeps on turning. Seeing the success of others is very good for the soul.

This is not just a women-for-women project; it has nothing to do with gender. Of course, I enjoy promoting and helping women. Diversity and equality are always in the back of my mind. But just as I benefited from mentorship and championship from the opposite sex, which enriched my professional and personal life, I equally champion and mentor people of all genders and backgrounds. That's doesn't matter, I want them to succeed, and I want to give them my time. It's a cycle. Had I been on my own, left to my own devices, and not benefited from these champions and mentors, would it come so naturally for me to do the same? Probably not.

The more people model this behavior, the more natural paying it forward becomes for future generations. It's a wheel that will keep on turning from that perspective, both professionally and personally.

It comes naturally for me to want to pay it forward because I was on the other end of the spectrum. I am who I am because of people like the parents who paid for my figure skating lessons and my physiotherapy, which led to me wanting to help other athletes, dancers, or boxers who needed funding. I was in their shoes once, so I get it.

I've also provided behind-the-scenes support, anonymously assisting those in need—for example, purchasing a dress for a dancer who couldn't afford one. You don't need credit for helping; just do it. It feels even better when no one knows it was you. I feel very strongly that because I received so much help in my life, openly and secretly, I want to do the same, and I want those I now help to eventually do the same. We say that hurt people, well, they hurt people; it's the same with kindness—it brings kindness.

When I became a board member of the Salvation Army, giving back to the organization that had helped me when I needed it the most felt natural. The big bow on top of paying it forward symbolizes the extra gift of nourishing your soul. I don't do it because I feel obliged to give back. It just makes me feel good. I don't think you can have a fulfilling, successful life if it's all about your own success. You can have it all, but you can also be happy by just being a good human being. There's a well-roundness that comes with kindness as you pay it forward.

From a professional standpoint, it is precisely because the Advocates' Society had been instrumental in helping me find my sea legs when I arrived in Toronto that I wanted to give back and get involved. I wanted others to benefit from this. That's why I became a board member and advocated for the Society to open a Quebec division. The Advocates' Society had been so good to me, so my immediate thought was, how can I get all the lawyers in Quebec to benefit from this great organization?

It wasn't just about me. I gained from this experience, and others needed to gain from it as well. It was about giving back to the profession as a whole. Training other trainers in Quebec who could then train more young lawyers became a full-circle moment from the very first time I got involved with the Society in Toronto.

The importance of collegiality also played a significant role. I had seen firsthand how the Society could impact one's career as a litigator, and I wanted my fellow Quebec litigators to benefit from this. Yes, it requires a lot of time and effort over and above your professional and personal responsibilities, but it is so worth it. The Quebec division of the Society is now thriving under the skillful leadership of others. It's wonderful to see, and it's good for my soul.

Some people perceive being generous or kind as a weakness, or as something that will take away from their hard-fought successes. This is simply false. And then there's that belief that they don't have the time to give back. "I have a family, children, and I'm involved in so many things." People ask how I do it all or call me the Energizer bunny. Yes, I have a lot of energy, but I worked on that all my life too. I've always had a lot of energy.

Many people claim they don't have time to do charity work, but my answer is that you need to find the time. Kindness and paying it forward must be part of your life. Even a small act can make a difference, and as time goes on, you may have more time to give. The key takeaway here is the importance of occasionally dedicating some of your time to doing something completely selfless.

Aim to do one good deed a day. It could be giving your time to a junior member of your team, making a phone call to help someone, or even serving on the board of an organization you care about. Overall, on a yearly basis, there needs to be something. It's like budgeting: you have your essential expenses, and then your long-term goals such as tuition funds for the kids or travel plans, and then your savings. Just like your short-, medium-, and long-term goals are part of your life plan, there should be a place for giving back. This balance is essential for success, fulfillment, and happiness.

As lawyers, we are given many opportunities to give back to society. One important way is pro bono work. Most large law firms engage in a significant amount of pro bono work each year, representing the most vulnerable at no cost, often in discrimination or Charter of Rights and Freedoms cases. When your day-to-day practice involves representing corporate clients in million-, or sometimes billion-dollars cases, few emotions are involved. While these are still important and complex cases, they rarely touch your soul. Doing pro bono work balances this out. Representing individuals in need is a vocation, and I have a great deal of admiration for my colleagues at the Bar who focus their careers on these types of cases.

It's in the context of one of these pro bono cases that the concept of giving back and paying it forward was taken to a completely different level for me. The *Mandy Bujold v. International Olympic Committee* case profoundly changed me. It was definitely good for my soul and ended up being the biggest case of my career. It was one of the most demanding, but also the most rewarding, emotionally. My team and I took on on this fight not just for Mandy, but for all female athletes in the world. It was one of those defining moments in life that you never, ever forget.

In 2020/21, when everyone believed the world was going to crumble amidst a global slowdown, lawyers were busier than ever. It often meant sixteen-hour days working on the computer from home. If there was a time when I could have said to Mandy, "Sorry, I'm just too busy. I don't have time, it's too intense right now," it would have been then, but her case was too big and too important. While I had a personal connection to Mandy, being a friend and my daughter's boxing coach, I would still have taken her case on if she had been a stranger because the issue was just too significant.

Olympian Mandy Bujold was the most decorated female boxer in Canada at the time. She had already competed at the Olympics in Rio in 2016 and had planned her entire life around going to the Tokyo Olympics in 2020. Her goal was to have a child in between those four years, which was a perfect plan. Immediately after Rio, she got married and became pregnant. Her daughter was born right on time in 2018. Mandy took the required one-year postpartum, retrained, won the Canadian nationals in 2019, and was on her way to the 2020 Continental Qualifier to win her spot in Tokyo. That's when things started going sideways because of the COVID-19 pandemic.

Mandy had a great team of professionals around her—sports psychologists, doctors, and coaches. She had done everything right, followed the rules, and was a medal hopeful. Her love for the sport and the Olympics was so profound that she named her daughter Kate Olympia, the initials being KO (knock out).

The Olympics were postponed to 2021. In April 2021, the Americas Continental Olympic Qualifier was canceled, and Mandy found out she'd been disqualified from competing in the Tokyo Olympics because of an unfair retroactive amendment to the qualification rules, which was, at its core, discrimination based on sex. All other continents—Africa, Australia, and Europe—had their qualifiers. All the other boxers fought for their spots according to the rules. For the Americas, the International Olympic Committee (IOC) decided that because they couldn't hold the qualifier event, they retroactively changed the rules and awarded points to boxers based on certain past events. The events they chose for the women were those during which Mandy had been pregnant or postpartum, resulting in her ending up with zero points and thus disqualified.

My field is not sports law. I didn't even know anything about sports law at the time. The Court of Arbitration for Sports (CAS) in Switzerland wasn't a court I was familiar with either. They had different rules, practices, and legal regimes, not to mention being in a foreign country. Nothing was familiar to me and my team. Despite many people telling us our legal challenge probably wouldn't work, and that we were facing an uphill battle, my team and I never doubted our ability to win. We never questioned whether we should take the case.

We sought advice from people who practiced in sports law, but not because we were secondguessing ourselves. The more people—mostly men—told us we couldn't take on the IOC, the more motivated we became. This was discrimination based on sex, without accommodations for pregnancy, so we needed to take it on for Mandy and all female athletes.

There were two significant problems with the retroactive change to the qualification rules. The qualifying period for men was longer, whereas it was only eleven months for women. If a woman was pregnant or postpartum during the eleven-month period, she was out of luck. There was no accommodation for women and no recognition of pre-pregnancy rankings. The fact that Mandy was one of the top boxers in the world before her pregnancy was irrelevant.

When Mandy called me, she said, "I'm done." Tokyo was going to be her last Olympics, as she planned to have a second child after Tokyo and then retire because she was in her 30s. She'd trained hard for the Tokyo Olympics, followed all the rules, and planned her entire life around it, only to be disqualified because she had zero points.

She asked me to look at the letter she had received. To me, it was discrimination based on sex. Surely the IOC didn't really realize the consequences of the retroactive rule. We were simply going to send a letter alerting them that this new rule discriminated against women who were legally entitled to accommodations. I was absolutely convinced that this letter would be enough.

After all, the IOC president had publicly stated that Tokyo was going to be the most gender-equal

Olympics of all times. In light of that media campaign, we naively believed they'd be receptive and provide accommodations to allow fair qualification for women. Unfortunately, the IOC completely ignored us, lending credit to those who'd warned us not to take them on. However, we did anyhow, and then it went *boom*!

The *New York Times* ran the story. On Mother's Day 2021, Mandy was on the front page of the sports section. We didn't see the wave of support from all over the world coming at all. Women could relate because similar situations had happened to them too. Some shared that, one week after a cesarean, they had to go back to training, otherwise they'd have lost their qualification. Others couldn't breastfeed because of training restrictions.

Moving forward with the case became very time-consuming because it had become an international story about women's rights. We suddenly had the weight of the world on our shoulders because it wasn't just about Mandy anymore. It became extremely stressful for me and my team. While it was the most emotionally demanding case of my career, by far, it also quickly became the most rewarding.

I put my life on hold for four months, living and breathing that case every minute of every day, as did my team. Without them, I never could have taken the case on. We had a large team, but my partner Sarah Whitmore was definitely my closest partner in crime in this venture. Sarah worked day and night with me. She had two young boys at home and didn't tell me she was pregnant with her third child during that crazy period. She refused to share the news because she was afraid I'd protect her and get her off the case, believing the stress and long hours were not something a pregnant woman should endure. So, she hid it from me—sneaky, indeed. However, she made a choice because that case took on a completely different significance for her. She conducted the best cross-examination of a witness I have ever seen. It was truly something straight out of a movie.

This was Mandy's greatest fight, and certainly mine as well. My colleagues had to chip in to support the rest of my practice, and Paul had to hold the fort at home. It became something so much bigger than just a phone call from Mandy on April 13, 2021.

It quickly became a case that I felt I could not afford to lose, and that was the driving force. There were no ifs, ands, or buts. This case was unlike any other; it left me emotionally spent and brought me to tears. After Mandy's closing statement at the end of the court hearing, there wasn't a dry eye in the room on our side.

The case wasn't about me, my goals, or money. I was entirely driven by doing what was right. With the support of the firm, I seized the opportunity because it was the right thing to do, and in the end, it became the most rewarding gesture of my life. It was good for my soul. In the beginning, I had no idea how it would affect me. I was fortunate that the culture at the firm allowed my colleagues to devote so many resources to the case over those four months. It was simply that important to do. The act of paying it forward was about creating opportunities for generations of female athletes to come.

We won and created an important precedent for female athletes. Mandy went to Tokyo, and then, as planned, had her second child.

Giving back and doing something for others does not hinder your success. Choose to do what's right. Choose to be kind. It will not negatively affect your reputation.

Other people might have passed on this case solely based on the amount of time it took, possibly fearing it would have a negative effect if they lost. This case awakened a sense of duty in me—a duty to women still striving today for equality, especially athletes. After our victory, I received many calls from women asking me about governance and maternity policy in sports. It also led me to accept other sport-related charity work. I needed to continue doing things that were good for my soul.

The same motivation led me to join the Toronto Advisory Board of the #Bravetheway campaign at the University of Montreal. What a way to pay it forward! This was the university that accepted me into the law program at nineteen years old on a scholarship. It mobilized law firms to provide scholarships, which led to me winning the Ogilvy Renault scholarship after my first semester. The rest is history, but it paved my way to success and where I am now. This was the university that allowed the "little girl from Beloeil" to pursue a higher education despite having no financial means. I didn't bat an eye when they asked me to help, even though the request came while I was trying to scale back and prioritize my well-being. In my book, this was the ultimate pay-it-forward gesture. I couldn't say no.

You need to incorporate acts of kindness, but in ways that create meaningful change. It doesn't need to be something as high profile as taking on an international legal battle. For some people, it's getting involved at their kids' school. If you are mid-career and want to be successful in your professional and personal life, this is another important component of that success. It's not just about family and career, as there's a third component to leading a happy, fulfilling life. Focusing solely on personal gain isn't a recipe for long-term satisfaction.

When you die, no one will remember what cases you won, what meetings you attended, or how much money you made. What will people say about you at your funeral? Doing something selfless adds to your life. Don't discount the effect of being selfless. When I've been someone's champion or mentor, and see them succeed, it's a great feeling—a very fulfilling feeling.

It's all a cycle. No matter what career path you take, you can help foster the next generation of champions, mentors, and caring individuals. People will emulate your behavior. It's very important to me to ensure the cycle of kindness and paying it forward continues with the next generation, because without it, I would never have reached my goals.

PRACTICAL TAKEAWAYS

Who is included in your support network, professionally and personally? Make a list and then add to it. Ensure you have enough supporters.

_____

_____

What does "having it all" mean to you?

_____

_____

Make a list of things that nourish your soul. Include those things in your quarterly goals.

_____

_____

Make gratitude journaling a daily practice.

_____

_____

CONCLUSION

This book is not an autobiography. That would be a very different project—one I may tackle in the future. I left out many important and interesting aspects of my life, not because they weren't worth mentioning; on the contrary, they simply weren't relevant to the life lessons I wanted to share under the overarching theme of "ownership." The idea for this book arose from a deep desire to help others—especially women—achieve happiness and fulfillment in their professional and personal lives.

Each chapter of this book includes stepping-stones to help you understand the importance of taking ownership of your life and learning how to achieve your goals. I wrote it to serve as a guide with strategies for unlocking your full potential in times of self-doubt. A guide is a valuable resource you can refer to over and over again, as needed.

I focused on eight life lessons based on my own experiences as a woman with an uncertain origin, a modest and occasionally difficult upbringing, and an adult life full of unexpected twists and turns. These lessons were essential in leading me to a successful and happy professional and personal life.

Do not let **Imposter Syndrome** halt your progress. Your past does not define you. Do not confine yourself to the limits of what you think you're allowed to be.

Be the **Master of your Own Destiny**. Take control of your life by making deliberate choices. Only you can decide what needs to be done, and when, to achieve your personal and professional goals. And yes, there will be plenty of times when making a choice is difficult. Such choices may cost friends, family, or partners, but you must still make them. Let go of anything that distracts or prevents you from reaching your objectives.

Step outside your Comfort Zone. Fear can be incredibly powerful. It can immobilize you, trapping you in what you know or what you're familiar with. Comfort—the word—sounds so cozy, warm, and safe. It's what we run to for solace, and that can be okay. We all need it once in a while, but don't linger there for too long. Don't shy away from opportunities because they make you uncomfortable. Engage in conversations, take on challenges, and discover new ways of doing things, even if it makes you uncomfortable. Become friends with being uncomfortable. Make it a familiar feeling. By pushing through your comfort zone, you will grow and evolve, leading you to success.

Ignore the White Noise. As the saying goes, everyone has an opinion, and you will get them from everyone. Once you strengthen your bond with your inner voice and instincts, these external voices will take a backseat, becoming mere white noise. Recognize those who believe in you and understand their motives for giving you advice or warning you. You are not invincible, and sometimes people will want to save you from yourself. Over time, you will get to distinguish who is truly supportive. If you know something can be done and your trusted guides agree, don't listen to the naysayers, as they'll tell you it's impossibly simply because they couldn't achieve it. Remember, their limitations do not define your potential.

Find **Champions and Mentors**. They are essential. No one can do it all alone. Seek people who believe in you and have the connections and knowledge to give you the upper hand. Those are the people who can lift you to the next level of success. In your search for champions and mentors, do not act as though you are superior or more deserving than others; entitlement is unbecoming. A champion will help you because they have faith in your work and character. Remember, they're putting their own name on the line for you. Deliver on your promises. Every single time. If you can't deliver, be open, honest, and humble.

Accept that **Life is a Marathon, not a Race**. Stay focused. Nothing worthwhile in life comes easily. It is true that it's the journey, not the destination, that matters. Every moment of hard work strengthens your discipline. Resilience and a strong work ethic will shape your character and prepare you for challenges throughout your life. Invest in yourself and your dreams. Through sheer will, you will make them a reality.

You Can Have It All. Plan, plan, and plan. Achieving goals requires intricate coordination. There are many moving parts: you need support from others and time. You have to be precise, and you'll have to prioritize the things that matter most. Allow everything else to fall by the wayside because there's no room for it, nor should there be. Fill your life with what's important to you—activities that bring you joy, challenge you, and allow you to balance your career with being a parent, sibling, spouse, or friend. Learn to let go of everything else. By weaving these elements together, you will have it all.

Lastly, **Be Grateful, Be Kind, and Pay it Forward**—always. By lifting others, you also rise. Life is about more than just monetary success or status. It's about the relationships you cultivate along the way. Remember those who helped you and those you can, in turn, help. We are all connected to one another, and you'll find that your experiences become richer when you give more than you take.

Your life is yours and yours alone.

Take ownership of who you are—your struggles, your decisions, and your future. Simply put: Own it!

www.ingramcontent.com/pod-product-compliance
Lightning Source LLC
Chambersburg PA
CBHW072157070526
44585CB00015B/1184